UNIVERSITY OF NORTH CAROLINA AT CHAPEL HILL
DEPARTMENT OF ROMANCE LANGUAGES

NORTH CAROLINA STUDIES
IN THE ROMANCE LANGUAGES AND LITERATURES

Founder: URBAN TIGNER HOLMES

Distributed by:

UNIVERSITY OF NORTH CAROLINA PRESS
CHAPEL HILL
North Carolina 27514
U.S.A.

NORTH CAROLINA STUDIES IN THE
ROMANCE LANGUAGES AND LITERATURES

Number 207

NARRATIVE PERSPECTIVE IN THE
POST-CIVIL WAR NOVELS OF FRANCISCO AYALA
MUERTES DE PERRO AND *EL FONDO DEL VASO*

NARRATIVE PERSPECTIVE
IN THE
POST-CIVIL WAR NOVELS
OF
FRANCISCO AYALA
MUERTES DE PERRO
AND
EL FONDO DEL VASO

BY

MARYELLEN BIEDER

CHAPEL HILL

NORTH CAROLINA STUDIES IN THE ROMANCE
LANGUAGES AND LITERATURES
U.N.C. DEPARTMENT OF ROMANCE LANGUAGES
1979

Library of Congress Cataloging in Publication Data

Bieder, Maryellen.
  Narrative perspective in the post-Civil War novels of Francisco Ayala, Muertes de perro and El fondo del vaso.

  (North Carolina studies in the Romance languages and literatures; no. 207)
  Bibliography: p.
  1. Ayala, Francisco, 1906- —Criticism and interpretation. 2. Ayala, Francisco, 1906- Muertes de perro. 3. Ayala, Francisco, 1906- El fondo del vaso. I. Title. II. Series.

PQ6601.Y3Z57   863'.6'2   78-32044
ISBN 0-8078-9207-6

I.S.B.N. 0-8078-9207-6

DEPÓSITO LEGAL: V. 740 - 1979   I.S.B.N. 84-499-2594-0
ARTES GRÁFICAS SOLER, S. A. - JÁVEA, 28 - VALENCIA (8) - 1979

I wish to acknowledge the Faculty Research Fellowship awarded by the SUNY Research Foundation in support of this study.

TABLE OF CONTENTS

	Page
INTRODUCTION	11
CHAPTER	
I. NARRATIVE PERSPECTIVE	21
II. *Muertes de perro*: THE SELF-CONSCIOUS NARRATOR DECEIVES HIMSELF	38
III. *El fondo del vaso*: THE UNCONSCIOUS NARRATOR REVEALS HIMSELF	71
A. Part I	72
B. Parts II and III	96
IV. IMPLIED AUTHOR AND READER COMMUNICATE	111
CONCLUSION	121
BIBLIOGRAPHY	128

INTRODUCTION

In reviewing a recent book on Francisco Ayala as theorist and practitioner of the art of literary creation, Keith Ellis, himself the first critic to undertake a broad analysis of Ayala's fiction, comments:

> In his most recent writings, ... it is clear that Ayala, whose powerful creative energy shows no sign of waning, is emphasizing a view of literary works as individual, delicate, coherent structures which, by their autonomy seem to demand study in the light of broad esthetic principles.... his literary criticism, his social and political thought and various aspects of his fiction deserve separate and thorough studies.[1]

The present study, which approaches the two novels comprising Ayala's major fictional work to date as individual, coherent structures and focuses on narrative perspective as a means of elucidating the techniques structuring the communication between author and reader, responds to the need signaled by Ellis for a thorough analysis of individual aspects of Ayala's fictional technique.

Now widely recognized as a major contemporary author, Francisco Ayala[2] is currently enjoying a resurrection in Spanish literary

---

[1] Rev. of *Teoría y creación literaria en Francisco Ayala,* by Estelle Irizarry, *Hispania,* 55 (1972), 970.

[2] Ayala's life and writings have already been adequately surveyed, first by Keith Ellis (*El arte narrativo de Francisco Ayala,* Madrid: Gredos, 1964) and more recently by Cecile Craig Fitzgibbon Wiseman ("*The Lamb's Head*: A Translation and Critical Study," Diss. Univ. of Texas 1971, pp. 1-21).

circles which have offered him steadily increasing critical acclaim [3] since his progressive reincorporation into the Spanish literary scene began in the late 1960's. Currently assigned a prominent position among Spanish men of letters, Ayala is considered a major figure of his literary generation and, together with Ramón Sender and the late Max Aub, one of the leading trio of exiled Spanish novelists. Reflecting both a consummate literary artistry and a constructively dissenting voice among the novels of social realism prevailing in Spain in the late 1950's and 1960's, Ayala's post-Civil War fiction was known first in Latin America, principally in Buenos Aires and in Puerto Rico, where he had resided since leaving Spain, and somewhat later in his most recent home, the United States.

Ayala's two post-Spanish Civil War novels, the interrelated novels *Muertes de perro* (1958) and *El fondo del vaso* (1962) [4] offer a two-dimensional perspective both on the narrators and events in a manner not dissimilar to that elaborated, in four-dimensional perspective, by Lawrence Durrell in his contemporaneous *Alexandria Quartet* (1957-1960) [5] or as less spectacularly employed by Joyce Cary in his first trilogy of the early 1940's. Ayala himself has declared of the link between the two novels that *El fondo del vaso* "surge en conexión con *Muertes de perro*. No es su segunda parte, pero sí secuela suya y — creo — superación." [6] Writing of Galdós' Torquemada novels, Ayala traces to Balzac the technique of introducing a lesser character from one novel into a later volume as a major character whose perspective differs from that presented in the earlier work, and has established its origins in Cervantes' masterpiece:

---

[3] This acclaim, according to the Spanish critic Antonio Iglesias Laguna (now deceased), comes from the critics' ulterior motive of furthering their own self-interests: "esta idea de que Francisco Ayala sea 'el primer novelista español' fue lanzada al ruedo por españoles interesados en ganarse los favores de Francisco Ayala," *Treinta años de novela española, 1938-1968*, I (Madrid: Prensa Española, 1969), p. 91.

[4] *Obras narrativas completas* (México: Aguilar, 1969). All references to Ayala's fiction through *El rapto* (1965) come from this edition.

[5] In a private correspondence, Ayala has affirmed: "Leí hace años el *Cuarteto de Alejandría*, de Durrell, pero debo confesarle que no me impresionó mayormente. Tendría que volverlo a leer para darme cuenta de por qué no me gustó demasiado"; 3 May 1972.

[6] *Mis mejores páginas* (Madrid: Gredos, 1965), p. 261.

El recurso, como es bien sabido, procede directamente de Balzac, que lo había usado de modo sistemático en *La Comedia Humana,* por cuyos diferentes cuerpos narrativos transitan, con mayor o menor relieve, los mismos personajes. Y no hay duda tampoco de que la introducción y empleo consecuente y deliberado de este recurso en la literatura novelesca se debe al autor del *Quijote,* cuyas dos partes no sólo lo aplican con mayor riqueza imaginativa, sino que lo extienden hasta el punto de acoger en sus páginas a un ente ficticio procedente de obra ajena: el caballero granadino que, desde el apócrifo, irrumpe en el mundo de nuestro don Quijote.[7]

As is frequently the case with the critical commentary of his own fiction, Ayala has been the first to voice this relationship between *Don Quijote* and the technique of interrelated novels.[8] Keith Ellis, however, rejects any comparison between the narrators of Balzac, Galdós or Durrell and José Lino Ruiz, the narrator of Ayala's novel *El fondo del vaso,* on the grounds of the absence of autonomy in their reappearance:

> The fact that the narrator used by Ayala en [sic] *El fondo del vaso* is consciously and explicitly motivated, as an autonomous character, by the desire to correct a previously given fictional account (in *Muertes...*) distinguishes him and the technique from [Galdós, Balzac and Durrell].[9]

The Swedish critic Bertil Romberg links this technique to the tradition of the English novel from the epistolary form to detective fiction:

---

[7] "Los narradores en las novelas de Torquemada," *La Nación,* 29 March 1970, Section 3, pp. 1, 3.

[8] Rosario Hiriart notes that she is the first to relate Ayala's use of this technique to the *Quijote*:

> La segunda parte de la novela cervantina se apoya, como *El fondo del vaso,* sobre la existencia real de la primera parte. El caballero manchego que sale a los caminos por tercera vez conoce por boca de Sansón Carrasco que su historia andaba impresa y el libro, que tiene existencia real, concreta, va a salirle una y otra vez al paso. También José Lino Ruiz, el personaje central de *El fondo del vaso,* tiene existencia anterior a la novela de la cual es personaje.

Los recursos técnicos en la novelística de Francisco Ayala (Madrid: Insula, 1972), pp. 72-73.

[9] Letter, 18 May 1972.

> The device of narrating the same material several times over from different points of view and with partially different emphasis links Durrell's tetralogy firmly to a venerable tradition inaugurated by Richardson's epistolary fiction, a tradition which, passing by way of Tieck and [Wilkie] Collins, for example, is still a much favoured method in the detective story.[10]

Romberg refers, of course, to the tradition of multiple perspectives within a single novel, whereas in the former examples — Cervantes, Balzac, Galdós, Durrell, Cary — the contrasting perspectives arise between successive interrelated novels. The device of re-narration from a new perspective superceding the previous one is not sustained throughout *El fondo del vaso*, the narrator's stated objective of presenting the "truth" which the first narrator has distorted being soon abandoned; thus the novel lies only partially within this august tradition. The link between the two novels, while not fundamental to the structure of the second novel, serves as the factor which initially motivates José Lino Ruiz to write his manuscript. Re-narration within a single novel, as in detective fiction, is fundamental to the structure of the first novel, *Muertes de perro*.

Responding to a question about his apparent abandonment of the novel form — since completing *El fondo del vaso* a decade ago Ayala has limited his attention to shorter fictional pieces — Ayala has clearly expressed his concern with technique as a motivating factor in his literary creativity:

> no le encuentro yo sentido a repetir fórmulas literarias, ni siquiera mis propias fórmulas, y cada vez que emprendo una obra nueva me propongo nuevos problemas literarios y persigo las técnicas adecuadas para resolverlos, en lugar de repetirme. Es mi concepto de la actividad creadora en arte, y de ahí la relativa parvedad de mi obra imaginativa. Comprenderá fácilmente que, de otro modo, me hubiera resultado factible escribir una docena de novelas análogas a *Muertes de perro*, o cualquiera de las otras.[11]

---

[10] *Studies in the Narrative Technique of the First-Person Novel*, trans. Michael Taylor and Harold H. Borland (Lund, Sweden: Almquist and Wiksell, 1962), p. 307.

[11] Antonio Núñez, "Francisco Ayala, más cerca," *Cuadernos para el Diálogo*, Extraordinario, No. 22 (Oct. 1970), rpt. in Francisco Ayala, *Confrontaciones* (Barcelona: Seix Barral, 1972), p. 79.

Ayala's conscious manipulation of narrative perspective, his concern with structure and his consummate literary craftsmanship, which the present study elucidates, make his novels ideally suited among contemporary Spanish novels for a searching analysis of the implications for the reader of the choice and handling of narrative perspective.

The techniques of narrative perspective in Ayala's fiction have not passed unnoticed by previous critics beginning with Keith Ellis' initial study, although the first novel, *Muertes de perro,* has received much greater critical attention than the later volume. Ellis has signaled the demand which the earlier novel's multiple, shifting perspectives make on the reader, concluding:

> el lector se ve forzado a tomar parte activa en el proceso creador de la novela. Ha de estar siempre alerta para captar el significado íntimo de la información que de cada suceso se le ofrece y poder apreciar de ese modo cómo se van complementando unos a otros los diversos acaecimientos hasta formar un cuadro completo. [12]

José-Carlos Mainer has raised, but then failed to answer, the question of "el arduo problema de la funcionalidad ética de la estructura 'primera persona'" in Ayala's fiction.[13] The same critic has also listed among the "keys" of Ayala's literary art "la cuidadosa selección de perspectivas o puntos de vista."[14] In a recent volume which considers Ayala's critical writings (up to but not including his lucid and concise *Reflexiones sobre la estructura narrativa*) in juxtaposition to his fictional works, Estelle Irizarry devotes a section to surveying "perspectiva y punto de vista" throughout Ayala's literary career, as one of five aspects singled out for concentrated attention. Irizarry views Ayala's widespread use of first-person narration in the context of his literary criticism, concluding about one of his critical studies:

---

[12] Ellis, *El arte narrativo de Francisco Ayala,* p. 200. Ellis does not discuss the reader's role in the second novel although he does describe the pervading irony.

[13] "La primera persona narrativa en Francisco Ayala y Serrano Poncela," *Insula,* 22, No. 242 (Jan. 1967), 3.

[14] "Prólogo" to Francisco Ayala, *Cazador en el alba y otras imaginaciones* (Barcelona: Seix Barral, 1971), p. 14.

> Este estudio tan perceptivo del manejo del punto de vista para cambiar la perspectiva, revela el interés de Ayala en el papel y la posición del personaje por cuyos ojos el lector ve el espectáculo. Ayala está siempre muy consciente de la cuestión del "narrador-espectador" en la ficción, y en sus novelas reiteradamente utiliza la conciencia de un personaje ínfimo para presentarnos ciertas perspectivas de la realidad. A veces el narrador-espectador se nos presenta al principio del relato, caracterizándose y explicándonos sus antecedentes, pero otras veces nos sorprende al final con su presencia inesperada para dejarnos saber que en realidad no hemos estado presenciando la historia de primera mano.[15]

Although *Muertes de perro* receives preponderant consideration in this section of Irizarry's study, the question of the reader's perspective on the novel remains untouched.

To date the most detailed consideration of narrative perspective in Ayala's recent novels is contained in Monique Joly's article, "Sistemática de perspectivas en *Muertes de perro*," which considers Ayala's first post-Spanish Civil War novel "una novela muy elaborada y estructurada."[16] Like Ellis, whom she cites, Joly points to the demands which the novel makes on the reader:

> nos exige un cierto trabajo de colaboración que impide toda pasividad. A diferencia de lo que ocurre con otros experimentos en el campo de la novela, la colaboración es aquí más que una sugerencia, es una imposición, so pena de abandonar la lectura.
>
> El lector que se presta a este juego queda tanto más satisfecho de los avances de su lucidez cuanto que a menudo las informaciones que recibe le son ofrecidas como secretos que pocos poseen.... Y así el lector se encuentra en una posición de superioridad con relación a ciertos personajes de la novela que no conocen más que una parte de la realidad.[17]

Joly, however, does not consider these "juegos de perspectiva" in the larger context of the communication between author and reader,

---

[15] *Teoría y creación literaria en Francisco Ayala* (Madrid: Gredos, 1971), p. 191.
[16] *Cuadernos Hispanoamericanos*, No. 245 (May 1970), p. 415.
[17] Ibid., p. 417.

and further overlooks the reader's superiority to all of the novel's characters who possess only a partial view of reality, as indeed of necessity does also the reader. By concentrating on the process and the order in which the reader acquires his knowledge, in contrast to the characters' more limited awareness, Joly does not view the reader's superior knowledge in relation to the author's ironic stance nor to the manner in which the author guides the reader's response to the text. Thus the focus of the present study of narrative perspective in Ayala's two novels falls within virtually unmapped critical territory: the ramifications of perspectivistic interplay within the total structure of the novel.

This study of Ayala's two major novels draws on four fundamental critical studies to support its critical framework in terms of narrative structure, first-person narration and definitions of irony. Among the studies directed toward detailing the functioning and implications of narrative point of view which have emerged in the past decade as seminal works, Wayne Booth's *The Rhetoric of Fiction* offers the fullest consideration of narrative perspective in the larger context of the techniques of communication in non-didactic fiction. The basic critical assumptions and vocabulary underlying this study of *Muertes de perro* and *El fondo del vaso* derive from Booth's analysis. In its survey of the techniques through which the author communicates with his reader, *The Rhetoric of Fiction* distinguishes the roles which enter into the communication process: "In any reading experience there is an implied dialogue among author, narrator, the other characters, and the reader."[18] These distinctions are fundamental to the present study which attempts to define the dimensions of each communicant's role in the implicit dialogue in Ayala's two novels.

Published within a year of Booth's study but presenting a much more limited scope, Bertil Romberg's *Studies in the Narrative Technique of the First-Person Novel* offers a systematic and more detailed, if also somewhat normative, consideration of the first-person narrator than *The Rhetoric of Fiction,* which explicitly subordinates the study of point of view to that of plot construction viewed as

---

[18] *The Rhetoric of Fiction* (Chicago: Univ. of Chicago Press, 1961), p. 155; hereafter cited as *Fiction.*

rhetoric.[19] In conjunction with Booth, Romberg represents a valuable overview from which to approach the first-person narrative of Ayala's novels. Since the narrators constitute the primary link in the chain of communication between author and reader, the analysis of each narrator's point of view forms the first step in the study which follows. An additional critical text, Francisco Ayala's slim volume of *Reflexiones sobre la estructura narrativa*, originally published in 1969 as a series of newspaper articles, argues in a manner similar to Booth's that literature is in essence communication between author and reader:

> Como cualquier otro escrito, la obra de arte literaria es — dicho queda — una comunicación cuya estructura presenta el mismo esquema básico de todo uso de lenguaje: arranca de un hablante (el autor) que comunica un contenido (el texto) a un destinatario (el lector u oyente).[20]

Ayala's brief but succinct text, which draws principally from Spanish literature in contrast to the broader literary traditions brought to bear in both Booth's and especially Romberg's studies, enters into consideration here only insofar as it complements or differs from the two other critical volumes and contributes an additional perspective from current Spanish literary criticism.

The other two critical works which underlie this study of Ayala's novels are D. C. Muecke's treatise on irony, *The Compass of Irony*, complemented by his brief monograph on the same subject, and Wayne Booth's more recent volume entitled *A Rhetoric of Irony*.[21] The different critical orientations of these two critics are indicated by the titles of their studies: the former offers a historical survey and classification of the kinds of irony from the perspective of the

---

[19] For a discussion by Booth of his emphasis on this larger context of plot construction viewed as rhetoric see, "*The Rhetoric of Fiction* and the Poetics of Fiction," *Novel*, 1 (1967-1968), rpt. in Wayne Booth, *Now Don't Try to Reason with Me* (Chicago: Univ. of Chicago Press, 1970), p. 165.

[20] *Reflexiones sobre la estructura narrativa* (Madrid: Taurus, 1970), p. 29, originally published as a series under the same title in *La Nación*, Section 4, 11 May 1969, 29 June 1969, 27 July 1969, 31 Aug. 1969, 5 Oct. 1969, and 25 Jan. 1970.

[21] D. C. Muecke, *The Compass of Irony* (London: Methuen, 1969), and *Irony*, The Critical Idiom, No. 13 (London: Methuen, 1970); and Wayne C. Booth, *A Rhetoric of Irony* (Chicago: Univ. of Chicago Press, 1974), hereafter cited as *Irony*.

ironist, while the latter undertakes a rhetorical inquiry into the process of communication between ironist and reader. An examination of the role of irony in *Muertes de perro* and *El fondo del vaso* completes the study of narrative perspective by focusing on the reader-author link in the communication chain which builds through the first-person narratives.

Published a decade ago and recipient of wide critical acclaim in the United States and England, *The Rhetoric of Fiction* has only recently been available in translation [22] and hence is largely absent from discussions of narrative perspective by Spanish critics. [23] Even Ayala's recent study of narrative structure has received little attention, although the broad outlines of his presentation are to be found in many of his earlier critical essays. Thus the incorporation of such major critical texts as *The Rhetoric of Fiction* into the present study of Ayala's novels in itself adds a new dimension to the study of the contemporary Spanish novel.

This study of narrative perspective in Ayala's two interrelated post-Spanish Civil War novels is presented in four chapters. The first chapter discusses the critical concepts and vocabulary underlying the analysis of *Muertes de perro* and *El fondo del vaso* which forms the major portion of the study. This critical framework is drawn from the three major critics already introduced: Wayne Booth, Bertil Romberg and, for the discussion of irony, D. C. Muecke. The central two chapters treat in turn the multiple narrative perspectives of each novel, focusing on the narrators as communicants

---

[22] In a letter dated 21 August 1975, Estelle Stinespring, Manager of Rights and Permissions for the University of Chicago Press, reports having licensed *The Rhetoric of Fiction* for translation into five languages. The Spanish edition, published by Editorial Bosch, appeared in 1975, as did the German and Italian editions; no French translation has been authorized. Booth's article entitled "Distance and Point-of-View: An Essay in Classification," published in *Essays in Criticism*, 11 (1961), 60-79, which in slightly revised form constitutes Chapter Six of *The Rhetoric of Fiction*, has been translated into French; "Distance et Point de Vue. Essais de classification," *Poètique*, 4 (1970), 511-24.

[23] Two critical studies published recently have outlined Booth's distinction between author, implied author and narrator without, however, implementing the distinction. Germán Gullón draws his discussion from *The Rhetoric of Fiction* in "La retórica de Cortázar en *Rayuela*," *Insula*, 26, No. 299 (Oct. 1971), 13. Santos Sanz Villanueva cites only Booth's article in French translation; *Tendencias de la novela española actual* (Madrid: Cuadernos para el Diálogo, 1972), pp. 238-39.

with the reader. The final chapter carries this analysis to its climax by treating the irony in each novel as the principal means through which the author communicates with the reader. Although in first-person narration all communication occurs through the voice of a narrator, the reader may detect irony on two levels — either within the narrative voice, if the narrator is himself an ironist, or over the head of the narrator, in which case the implied author is the nominal ironist. The recognition of irony in this latter case requires the active participation of the reader in the communication process. The position of the author relative to the worldview expressed in each novel emerges from this communication between reader and author. The conclusion of this study views both the role of the reader and the emergent vision of the novelistic world of *Muertes de perro* and *El fondo del vaso* in the context of earlier critical commentary, pointing to the contributions of the present study in elucidating the communication process between narrator, reader and author which constitutes a work of literature. The study demonstrates Ayala's mastery of narrative technique and his skillful, controlled manipulation of narrative perspective and reader response, which make these two contemporary Spanish novels an excellent medium for such an in-depth examination of communication in fiction.

CHAPTER I

NARRATIVE PERSPECTIVE

A. *Spain*

Contemporary critical concern with narrative perspective in English fiction dates principally from Henry James and the principal exponent of his narrative technique, Percy Lubbock.[1] In Spanish criticism discussion of narrative perspective in artistic creation can be traced to the theories of José Ortega y Gasset, the leading intellectual force in the literary and philosophical circles during Ayala's days as a student and then professor at the University of Madrid. In his publication *El espectador*, Ortega expressed himself as the detached spectator of society whose emblematic presence at the Escorial constituted his personal perspective on man. Introduced first into his University lectures in 1913 and frequently raised in the articles of *El espectador*, Ortega's "doctrina del perspectivismo" rested on his assertion that: "El punto de vista individual me parece el único punto de vista desde el cual mirarse el mundo en su verdad."[2] Ortega incorporated his theory into *El tema de nuestro tiempo* in a chapter on "La doctrina del punto de vista."[3] His elaboration of the theory in relation to artistic creativity came in the now familiar chapter of *La deshumanización del arte*, published

---

[1] Bruce Morrissette traces the term "point of view" to 1866 and an anonymous critic writing in the *British Quarterly Review*; "De Stendhal à Robbe-Grillet: Modalités du 'Point de vue,'" *Cahiers de l'Association Internationale des Etudes Françaises*, No. 14 (March 1962), p. 144.

[2] "Verdad y perspectiva," in *Obras completas*, II: *El espectador (1916-1934)* (Madrid: Revista de Occidente, 1946), p. 18.

[3] *Obras completas*, III (Madrid: Revista de Occidente, 1947), pp. 197-202.

in the same year as Francisco Ayala's first novel. "Unas gotas de fenomenología" contrasts the individual perspectives of each of four persons present at the bedside of a dying man: his wife, his doctor, a journalist and an artist. The differentiating factor is distance: "la distancia espiritual a que cada uno se halla del hecho común, de la agonía."[4] At the same time that Ortega was expounding his new theory of perspectivism, Ramón Pérez de Ayala was experimenting, in a somewhat artificial manner, with incorporating the same principle into his novels. A brief section of *Troteras y danzaderas*, appearing in the same year as Ortega's first lectures on *perspectivismo*, offers the reader in turn the contrasting points of view of each character present in a room. In his later novel *Belarmino y Apolonio*,[5] which antedates *El tema de nuestro tiempo*, a famous chapter presents the best-known example of Pérez de Ayala's technique, which the one Spanish critic to focus on this aspect of modern Spanish fiction has described as "esencialmente estético y psicológico" in contrast to earlier literary examples of perspectivism "de intención más bien ética."[6]

Despite this interest in narrative perspective earlier in the century as manifested in a leading novelist and an influential literary critic, there has been a distinct paucity of point-of-view studies among critics of the contemporary Spanish novel. Whereas Booth, working in the tradition of English and American literature, could write of his *Rhetoric of Fiction*, "I set out in part to undermine those who would make manipulation of point-of-view the whole art of fiction,"[7] and Romberg could draw his critical vocabulary almost exclusively from German literary criticism, in Spain studies of narrative perspective remain minimal. A recent Spanish critic asserts that, "el factor 'punto de vista,' insólitamente ignorado hasta el medio siglo, está hoy generalmente reconocido. E incluso se la ha concedido una importancia próxima al extremismo."[8] Nevertheless, this interest in point of view has been generated largely in

---

[4] Ibid., p. 361.
[5] *Troteras y danzaderas* (Madrid: Biblioteca Renacimiento, 1913); *Belarmino y Apolonio* (Madrid: Calleja, 1921).
[6] Mariano Baquero Goyanes, *Perspectivismo y contraste: De Cadalso a Pérez de Ayala* (Madrid: Gredos, 1963), pp. 7-8.
[7] Booth, "Poetics of Fiction," p. 165.
[8] Sanz Villanueva, p. 239.

a normative, rather than an analytical, context. While critical studies drawing upon point of view are limited, the more recent development of interest in Spain in structural criticism is furthering the awareness of the importance of textual analyses, including studies of narrative perspective.

As both author and critic, Francisco Ayala may have contributed more than any other one figure to drawing the attention of the reading public in Spain, and to an even greater extent in Latin America, to the necessity for careful reading of the narrative perspective. That is, Ayala has been a strong voice favoring interpreting this communication on the basis of the text itself, rather than subordinating the text to the known facts of the author's life outside his fiction. To cite an example, Ayala has stated that the motivation to write the articles comprising *Reflexiones sobre la estructura narrativa,* which appeared originally in *La Nación,* came from his "polémica amistosa" with a critic over the interpretation of Ayala's introduction to *El rapto,* which the critic attempted to assign either to the "real" author Ayala, in which case Ayala had taken certain liberties in presenting himself to the public, or to a fictional narrator whose life bore an uncomfortable degree of similarity to Ayala's.[9]

B. *Critical Concepts*

As elaborated in *The Rhetoric of Fiction,* rhetoric reveals itself to be "the study of the art of persuasion," that is, of the persuasion which characterizes the communicative process between author and reader which lies at the heart of all literature.[10] The first step in analyzing this communication is to disassociate the historical man who is the acknowledged author of the text from the image which the author projects of himself within the text. Booth defines this implicit presence underlying the work of fiction as the "implied author," while acknowledging other similar terms such as the author's "second self,"[11] describing the process by which the author

---

[9] Francisco Ayala, "La relación entre el autor, el lector y el personaje en la obra narrativa," Lecture at the Univ. of Minnesota, 23 May 1970.

[10] Wayne Booth, "The Revival of Rhetoric," *PMLA,* 80, No. 2 (1965), rpt. in *Now Don't Try to Reason with Me,* p. 35.

[11] Booth accepts this term "second self" as employed by Kathleen Tillotson in *The Tale and the Teller* (London, 1959); *Fiction,* p. 71.

creates an implied self in each work of fiction he produces and its function for the reader:

> As he writes, he creates not simply an ideal, impersonal "man in general" but an implied version of "himself" that is different from the implied authors we meet in other men's works.... Our reactions to his various commitments, secret or overt, will help to determine our response to the work.[12]

Similarly, Ayala has more recently introduced the expression "autor ficcionalizado" into Spanish criticism:

> el autor queda ficcionalizado dentro de la estructura imaginaria que él mismo ha producido, aun en el caso de que aparezca en ella ostentando los caracteres de la más comprobable identidad personal.[13]

But whereas Booth does not stipulate that the various implied authors of a novelist's total fictional output are identical, Ayala finds consistency throughout a novelist's career:

---

[12] Booth, *Fiction,* pp. 70-71.

[13] Ayala, *Estructura,* pp. 22-29, 27. Romberg, on the other hand, does not differentiate between the flesh-and-blood author and the "autor ficcionalizado." Indeed, in making a distinction between "the 'I' that belongs to that figure in the novel who appears as the narrator, and the 'I' belonging to the novelist, the *author*," Romberg explicitly identifies the author with this latter 'I' as Ayala does not; Romberg, p. xi. Ayala, however, in a second definition of *autor ficcionalizado* appears to blur the distinction between narrator and implied author, defining "el autor ficcionalizado en el poema" as:

> el yo que habla, a quien en un sentido amplio podemos llamar narrador, puesto que en todo poema se dice algo, se cuenta de algún modo una historia.

p. 57.

Working from within an entirely different critical tradition than Booth, the Chilean critic Félix Martínez Bonati has arrived at a position similar to that of Booth and Ayala as regards the necessity of distinguishing between *autor empírico, autor ideal* and *hablante ficticio* as well as of establishing the role of the *lector ficticio* relative to the text. Trained in German phenomenology, Martínez Bonati has, of all the Spanish language critics, come closest to the critical stance of Booth and Ayala in the section on "Lenguaje y literatura" of his *La estructura de la obra literaria* (Santiago: Univ. de Chile, 1960), pp. 95-145.

> Pero — no lo olvidemos — detrás de éste, detrás del autor ficcionalizado que, según pudimos observar, se incorpora a cada obra de arte literaria como un elemento básico de su estructura, queda siempre el creador, el poeta, el espíritu libre, que acaso, objetivado en sus producciones, sobrevive por siglos, y que desde ellas nos habla tal vez con diferentes intenciones, temple y humor, pero con el mismo acento personal siempre, porque esas producciones, aún siendo autónomas como lo son, responden todas ellas a una sola y original visión del mundo: la de un individuo concreto.[14]

Booth does not postulate this consistency in an author's projection of himself throughout his writings because he does not relate the implied author's worldview to that of the "real" author as does Ayala. Indeed, Booth suspends all judgment as to the relationship between these two sets of values which he has so carefully separated for the purpose of approaching the text on its own terms. He thus does not share Ayala's concern with the reduction of these norms to their common denominator. A critic of Booth has based one of his major criticisms precisely on this point, arguing that "the norms and choices [Booth's definition at one point of the implied author] we know to underlie a novel are surely attributable to the *real* author." His defense is based largely on the fact of common practice: "we commonly leap out from our self-imposed category of discourse and talk about the author, imputing to him what we infer from his book."[15] On this point he is hardly at odds with Booth who offers a critical mechanism for avoiding the pitfalls of this practice, which the critic acknowledges, and assuring a reading of the novel grounded in the novel itself.

Nor has Ayala always paid tribute to the presence of the fictionalized author. In an early essay on *Muertes de perro* he wrote, overlooking the function of the author's "second self":

---

[14] Ayala, *Estructura*, p. 60. A few pages earlier Ayala makes the same clear distinction between the implied author of each text as does Booth, stating:

> si cada poema constituye una unidad singular, también es distinto en cada caso — incluso tratándose de dos obras escritas por la misma mano — el autor ficcionalizado en el poema.

p. 57.

[15] John Killham, "My Quarrel with Booth," *Novel*, 1 (1967-1968), 269.

> El autor está ausente siempre del recinto de la novela; no guía a sus lectores, ni les imparte sus propias opiniones o juicios; y esa abstención suya, al eliminar toda instancia mediadora, los obliga a envolverse y enredarse en la trama, cayendo en la trampa de la implicación.... el autor no los denuncia [a los personajes novelescos], el autor no dice nada.[16]

However, the implied author might well be defined precisely as an "instancia mediadora" which may not necessarily cause the reader to identify with the characters, unless the distance between characters and implied author is negligible. Essentially Ayala has greatly simplified the reader's response and downplayed the techniques through which an author manipulates this reader response. At the same time, Ayala does recognize the difference between a novelist's intentions and the finished work, acknowledging in effect the author's projection of himself, or second self, as distinct from his intended projection of himself.

In the discussion of Ayala's novels in the following chapters of this study, the implied author will be treated as the originator of the communication process. Ayala has already pointed to the propensity among critics to identify him, that is his personal experiences and ideas, with the characters of his novels:

> a las razones generales que entorpecen el entendimiento de una novela en su pretensión de obra artística vienen a sumarse en el caso de las mías circunstancias personales de donde arrancan nuevos equívocos.
>
> Ocurre, en efecto, que siendo bastante conocidos mis escritos de sociología y ciencia política, propenda el crítico de manera casi inevitable a querer ver incorporada en mis novelas la actividad o conocimientos de sociólogo, y así, busque las ideas tejidas en su trama.[17]

The present study recognizes the importance of identifying the implied author's "core of norms and choices" without reference to those of the real author or to those of the narrator or other characters, since the implied author guides the reader's response to the novel. If the reader fails to communicate with the implied author

---

[16] Francisco Ayala, "El fondo sociológico en mis novelas," *Cuadernos Hispanoamericanos*, No. 228 (Dec. 1968), p. 545.

[17] Ibid., p. 537.

as he reads, he will not be reading the work as it is written. Booth describes a "successful reading" in the following manner:

> The author creates ... an image of himself and another image of his reader; he makes his reader, as he makes his second self, and the most successful reading is one in which the created selves, the author and reader, can find complete agreement. [18]

Ayala terms this image of the reader created by the implied author "el lector ficcionalizado," describing him in a manner quite similar to Booth's conceptualization of him:

> cualesquiera sean sus demás características, el destinatario de la creación poética es también, como su autor, y como ella misma, imaginario; es decir, que se halla incorporado en su textura, absorbido e insumido en la obra. El lector a quien una novela o un poema se dirigen pertenece a su estructura básica, no menos que el autor que le habla, y está también incluido dentro de su marco. [19]

---

[18] Booth, *Fiction*, pp. 137-38. Wolfgang Iser also discusses the role of the "implied reader" in his collection of essays of the same title, defining the term as incorporating:

> both the prestructuring of the potential meaning by the text, and the reader's actualization of this potential through the reading process. It refers to the active nature of this process — which will vary historically from one age to another — and not to a typology of possible readers.

The Implied Reader: Patterns of Communication in Prose Fiction from Bunyan to Beckett (Baltimore: Johns Hopkins Univ. Press, 1974), p. xii. (While Iser does not establish the origin of the usage "implied reader," he does cite Booth in reference to the distinction between the "author who has written the novel" and the "*author's voice in fiction*"; p. 237.) Booth also takes into consideration the changing response to a text by succeeding generations of readers, although he stresses the common elements of "firmly grounded interpretations that all good readers share"; *Irony,* p. 126. Booth further stipulates that:

> the whole engagement between author and reader depends on a world they never made, and it depends, in summary, on at least three kinds of agreement: (a) their common experience of the vocabulary and grammar of [the language]...; (b) their common cultural experience and their agreement about its meaning and value...; (c) their common experience of literary genres, a potentially large (but almost certainly finite) number of shared grooves or tracks into which reading experience can be directed.

p. 100.

[19] Booth, *Fiction*, p. 33.

Since in his *Rhetoric of Fiction,* Booth does not consistently distinguish the "real" reader from the implied reader, the necessity to do so not being as fundamental to clarity as is the case with the author, "reader" will be understood to mean the fictionalized reader in this study as in Booth's.[20]

In both of Ayala's novels the communication between implied author and reader passes through a narrator, either a first-person narrator or, as in the case of the newspaper clippings in *El fondo del vaso,* a third-person narrator whose voice is identifiably unique and therefore also distinguishable from that of the implied author. In the case of these two novels, unlike *El rapto,* there is little likelihood of any reader identifying the author with the narrator of either volume, although in novels in which the distance between implied author and narrator is minimal, or in which the reader is led to make this identification on the basis of his "outside" knowledge of the "real" author's life, the distinction must be established. The key to the reader's response to a novel lies in the distance separating the narrator from the implied author and hence from the reader, distance which produces either identification in the form of sympathy or "implication," to use Ayala's term, or the opposite, rejection. Documents, diaries and conversations transmitted to the reader through the first-person narrator are in effect refracted through a second narrative consciousness which thus doubly distances them from the reader.

Booth enumerates five possible combinations of distancing in a novel, three of which derive from the nature of the narrator. The distance between narrator and implied author yields a reliable or unreliable narrator, narrating either self-consciously or unself-consciously; the distance between the narrator and the other characters, either a privileged or a limited narrator, either an agent or an observer; and the distance between the narrator and the reader's norms, a sympathetic or unsympathetic narrator. The most significant of these distance variables, in Booth's judgment, is the distance between the implied author and an unreliable narrator, that is, a narrator who does not speak for or act in accordance with

---

[20] In his later study, Booth consistently employs the term "implied reader" to designate the reader implicit within the text itself, as distinguished from the individual who is actively engaged in reading the work; *Irony,* p. 126.

the norms of the work.²¹ The distance between narrator and implied author does not in turn predicate the distance between the other characters and the implied author. Booth is prescriptive only as regards the fifth distance variable, the distance between implied author and reader, declaring that:

> From the author's viewpoint, a successful reading of his book must eliminate all distance between the essential norms of his implied author and the norms of the postulated reader.²²

It is precisely on this point that Ayala's critical comments concerning his novels would appear to differ with Booth's interpretation of the implied author-postulated reader relationship.

Ayala posits as a general effect deriving from first-person narration greater identification between implied author and reader, arguing that, when the author presents his characters from within:

> se complica él mismo y complica al lector en la existencia del personaje. Ya no podrán éstos sentirse ajenos a la suerte de aquéllos, superiores, sino que se sentirán hundidos en la común miseria.²³

Thus Ayala interprets first-person narration as establishing a minimum distance between narrator and implied author-reader. Here he appears to be in conflict with Booth, who shows that the implied author can also draw the reader away from identification with the narrator, obviating the complicity to which Ayala refers by aligning the reader in his implicit viewpoint. This the implied author accomplishes to a great extent through irony which distances the reader from the narrator's norms by establishing a frame of reference built of superior knowledge in which to judge the narrator, leading the reader to stand apart from the narrator's norms and accept instead those of the implied author. Taking *The Sound and the Fury* as an example, Booth details: "We delight in communion, even in deep collusion, with the author behind Jason's back." But even when the narrator is both unreliable and unsympathetic, as

---

²¹ Booth, *Fiction,* pp. 158-59.
²² Ibid., p. 157.
²³ Ayala, *Mis mejores páginas,* p. 19.

Jason obviously is, his very vulnerability creates a bond, such as the one Ayala writes of, even while the full effects of irony are in force; but the bond is still rooted in the superiority which is the keystone of irony. To continue with the earlier example:

> We watch with him [Faulkner] while this Vice reveals himself for our contempt, our hatred, our laughter, and even — so strong is the effect of his psychological vitality — our pity.[24]

Northrup Frye resolves this seeming conflict in reader distance in his definition of the fictional modes which he classifies according to the hero's power of action:

> If inferior in power or intelligence to ourselves, so that we have the sense of looking down on a scene of bondage, frustration or absurdity, the hero belongs to the ironic mode. This is still true when the reader feels that he is or might be in the same situation, as the situation is being judged by the norms of a greater freedom.[25]

Frye's definition places Ayala's two novels squarely within the ironic mode, as indeed it does "most serious fiction" written during the past hundred years, and offers a broader critical tradition within which to consider the reader's response to the narrator.

In sum, the narrator is the intermediary in the communication which comprises a work of literature; through him it encompasses the other characters and is received by the reader. Since it is the narrator whose role in the novel determines the distance which the reader must span to communicate with the implied author, an analysis of the techniques of narrative perspective incorporating all three participants forms the core of this study of Ayala's novels.

C. *Irony*

The distance separating the reader of Ayala's novels from the events narrated, a distance created both by the nature of the events themselves and the first-hand perspective from which they reach

---

[24] Booth, *Fiction*, p. 307.
[25] *Anatomy of Criticism* (1957; rpt. New York: Atheneum, 1965), p. 34.

the reader in most instances, allows, in Ayala's own terms, a "distanciamiento irónico" through which the reader adopts "una actitud desprendida y crítica." At the same time, however, again according to Ayala, the reader "debiera quedar envuelto por completo en la experiencia, emocional y no sólo intelectualmente."[26] Here the narrator is not the ironist but the unwitting transmitter of ironies perceived by the implied author and in turn by the reader. Writing of *El fondo del vaso,* Ayala comments: "muy bien pudieran subrayarse observaciones o sugestiones irónicas indicativas de una supuesta actitud crítica respecto del sistema."[27] This irony might derive either directly from the narrator as ironist or from the contrast between the narrator's words and the very circumstances described by him. Again, in the latter case, the narrator himself is unaware of the irony, although he is not himself necessarily the object of it.

Little critical attention has been paid to the large amount of irony implicit in Ayala's novels, aside from observations by the author and passing reference by critics, such as José-Carlos Mainer who includes it among the key elements of Ayala's fiction:

> la fascinación que la vulgaridad ejerce sobre el escritor y que le hace preferirla como óptica del relato [y] la zona de reserva irónica que Ayala se proporciona en este caso.[28]

Here Mainer limits Ayala's ironic vein to ironic characterization, while Ayala himself has cited the irony of events as well. José Marra-López also includes irony as one of the fundamental characteristics of Ayala's entire literary corpus, again without detailing its role.[29] Another critic, Enrique Pezzoni, has written of the

---

[26] "Nueva divagación sobre la novela," *Revista de Occidente,* 2ª serie, 18 (1967), 311-12.
[27] Ayala, "El fondo sociológico en mis novelas," p. 542.
[28] Mainer, "Prólogo," p. 14.
[29] *Narrativa española fuera de España, 1939-1961* (Madrid: Guadarrama, 1963), pp. 223, 268-72, 275. David A. Foltz, who includes a discussion of *El fondo del vaso* in a recent examination of alienation in four modern novels, refers periodically to the ironies in Ayala's novel, but he is using the term loosely, without defining the types of irony involved; "Beyond Alienation in Four Contemporary American Novels," Diss. Univ. of Arizona 1974, pp. 15, 25, 46, 49, *passim.*

reader's task in *El fondo del vaso* in terms of irony, but without specifying this ironic dimension:

> Se cierra el libro y tiene uno la impresión de que Ayala, guarecido tras sus disfraces lastimosos, se sonríe con sorna ante nuestro desconcierto. Nos ha dado las cifras, pero a nosotros corresponde el cuidado de encontrarles la clave.
> La lectura de la última novela de Ayala no es fácil: está destinada a quien pueda sentir otra curiosidad que la de una historia contada con argucia y con solución en la última página.[30]

Pezzoni has identified the configuration of the implied author, Ayala's second self, in this novel, but he has left unclarified the reader's comprehension of this stance. The reader is not only implicated in the structure of the novel; he must collaborate with the implied author to reach the "solution," shaping his perspective towards the work and his perception of its norms as he reads. One of the rewards of coinciding with the implied author in Ayala's fiction is that this detachment from the characters and events allows the reader to participate in the ironies.[31]

Thus a detailing of the reader's response to Ayala's fiction requires a consideration of Ayala's utilization of the techniques of irony resulting from the interplay of narrative perspectives, since when the reader joins with the implied author in distancing himself from the narrator, irony is a standard by-product:

> Whenever an author conveys to his reader an unspoken point, he creates a sense of collusion against all those, whether in the story or out of it, who do not get that point. Irony is always thus in part a device for excluding as well as for including.... In the irony with which we

---

[30] Enrique Pezzoni, "Francisco Ayala: La novela de la responsabilidad," *Sur*, No. 284 (Sept.-Oct. 1963), p. 91.

[31] In summarizing the author-reader relationship in stable irony, Booth asserts that the victims never include the implied author, "whatever victimized masks he assumed in passing," or "the true implied reader"; in short, "the reader and author were intended to stand after their work was done, firmly and securely together"; *Irony*, p. 233. In Booth's terminology, irony is stable when, "once a reconstruction of meaning has been made, the reader is not then invited to undermine it with further demolitions and reconstructions"; Ibid., p. 6.

are concerned [unreliable narration], the speaker is himself the butt of the ironic point. The author and reader are secretly in collusion, behind the speaker's back, agreeing upon the standard by which he is found wanting.[32]

Aside from overt verbal irony in which the narrator is a conscious ironist, two basic ironies emerge from Ayala's novels: verbal irony and situational irony. In verbal irony the implied author as ironist is being ironic behind the narrator's back, the narrator thus being the victim of the irony as perceived by the reader. In situational irony there is no ironist, but instead a victim and an observer; in Ayala's fiction the observer is either an ironic narrator-observer, as in *Muertes de perro,* or, if the characters themselves remain blind to the irony, the reader functions as the observer. When the first-person narrator is the victim of the irony, his words must convey to the reader both his own unawareness and the materials with which the reader, relying on the implied author, detects the irony. Muecke elaborates on the roles of victim and observer in describing one of the basic elements of irony, the element of "innocence" or "confident unawareness":

> The victim of irony does not need to be, though he often is, arrogantly, wilfully blind; he need only reveal by word or action that he does not even remotely suspect that things may not be what he ingenuously supposes them to be. The basic element is a serene, confident unawareness coloured, in practice, by varying degrees of arrogance, conceitedness, complacency, naivety, or innocence. Other things being equal, the greater the victim's blindness, the more striking the irony. It goes without saying that the ironic observer must be aware of the victim's unawareness as well as of the real situation.[33]

---

[32] Booth, *Fiction,* p. 304. In his later study Booth cautions:

> No matter how firmly I am convinced that a statement is absurd or illogical or just plain false, I must somehow determine whether what I reject is also rejected by the author, and whether he has reason to expect my concurrence.

Irony, p. 11. Booth is, of course, referring here to the implied author or "creative person responsible for the choices that made the work."

[33] Muecke, *Irony,* pp. 25, 28.

When the victim remains completely blind to the irony, the reader shifts from aligning himself with the ironist, as in verbal irony, or the ironic observer, and actively participates himself as the observer, reading in conjunction with the implied author.[34]

Muecke defines irony as "a double-layered or two-storey phenomenon":

> At the lower level is the situation either as it appears to the victim of irony (where there is a victim) or as it is deceptively presented by an ironist (where there is an ironist).... At the upper level is the situation as it appears to the observer or ironist. The upper level need not be *presented* by the ironist; it need only be evoked by him or be present in the mind of the observer. Nor need it be more than a hint that the ironist does not quite see the situation as he has presented it at the lower level ... or that the victim does not see the situation quite as it really is.[35]

One of the formal requirements for irony is an opposition between these two levels in the form of "contradiction, incongruity, or incompatibility."[36] The reader detects situational irony in the contradiction between a text and its larger context through foreknowledge or his superior level of awareness relative to the narrator, an awareness built up over a period of increasing disassociation from an unreliable narrator. The reader's superior understanding, which he shares with the implied author, leads him to detect simple incongruities of speech or action which the narrator blindly records. In these cases the ironies may be considered as created and presented by the implied author who thus becomes the ironist, the deployer of ironic situations. The implied author as ironist functions widely through dramatic irony which presents no visible ironist

---

[34] Booth breaks down the steps in the reconstruction of meaning by the reader as follows:

> a *required rejection* of the surface meaning; a consideration of *alternatives*; a *decision* about the author's position; and a *reconstruction* in harmony with what we infer about that position.... The details of our reconstruction will depend, of course, on how our knowledge and experience relate to the implied author's intention.

Irony, p. 147.
[35] Muecke, *The Compass of Irony*, p. 19.
[36] Ibid., pp. 19-20.

and which requires reader participation for it to become effective.[37] Muecke identifies two facets of dramatic irony:

> There is certainly a distinction to be made between a situation in which a man does not fully understand the meaning of the words he uses or hears and one in which he does not fully understand the situation he is in, but both are forms of Dramatic Irony.[38]

Irony is most easily perceived in an unreliable narrator whom the reader has learned to distrust; in distancing himself from the narrator's perspective, the reader places the fallible narration in a larger context in which the contrast reveals itself. Furthermore, according to Booth, the ironic pleasure is heightened "as we travel with less sympathetic protagonists whose faults are never described directly,"[39] as is certainly the case with first-person narration and especially with the principal narrators of Ayala's two novels.

In both of Ayala's novels the initial function of the narrative, according to each narrator, is to reveal the other characters to the reader in their "true" dimensions; however, a secondary result may

---

[37] David Worcester emphasizes the reader's role in detecting dramatic irony:

> In dramatic irony, the ringmaster [overt ironist] disappears. There is no signpost, not even a misleading one, to inform the spectators that irony is present. All the work of detection and interpenetration is left to them. There is no obligation to explore beneath the surface level of the narrative. As a result, everyone who does so is translated into a ringmaster on his own account.

The Art of Satire (1940; rpt. New York: Norton, 1969), p. 120. Booth, on the other hand, focuses on the role of the implied author and asserts that dramatic irony occurs:

> whenever an author deliberately asks us to compare what two or more characters say of each other, or what a character says now with what he says or does later. Any plain discrepancy will do, though it is true that conventions like the soliloquy or the epistolary technique in novels are especially useful because especially sure.

Irony, p. 63.

Muecke uses the metaphors of puppet and puppet-master to describe the relationship between the narrative voice which communicates the irony to the reader and the implied author as ironist-in-the-wings; *The Compass of Irony*, p. 45.

[38] Ibid., p. 106.
[39] Booth, *Fiction*, p. 306.

frequently outweigh the stated narrative intent in such cases, as Romberg details:

> when a narrator describes a main character from a lateral perspective ... the gaze of the narrator, fastened as it is upon the main character, simultaneously reflects the narrator himself. But it is the personality of the narrator that gives his story its characteristic colouring and cachet; often the information which the narrator gives unconsciously about himself is of greater interest than the information that he conveys as part of his conscious purpose. Thus, in this type of novel, the author has an opportunity to build up a contrast between narrator and main character, which gives the reader a dual perspective onto the action.[40]

When the narrator engages in unconscious, indirect narration, as described here, while believing himself to be relating directly and consciously information of a different nature, he is incurring the irony of unconscious self-betrayal in which characters unconsciously ironize themselves. In Muecke's words, "it is exemplified whenever someone, by what he says or does (not by what happens to him), exposes unawares his own ignorance, weaknesses, errors, or follies."[41] Similar to the irony of self-betrayal but relating to the circumstances in which the narrator finds himself, rather than to his self-ignorance, is the more commonly identified dramatic irony, in which the victim remains serenely unaware that the real state of affairs is quite different from what he assumes it is.

After analyzing the reader's response to the first-person narrator of each of Ayala's two novels, this study focuses on irony as a means of detailing the process of reader-implied author communication, which occurs either through the narrator's conscious narration, in those cases in which the narrator functions as the verbal ironist or the ironic observer, or through the unconscious narration of dramatic irony in which the implied author is the nominal ironist

---

[40] Romberg, p. 63.
[41] Muecke, *The Compass of Irony*, p. 107. According to Muecke, this kind of irony has only recently been distinguished by critics from the larger category of dramatic irony. Although the use of the irony of self-betrayal dates back to Fielding, Muecke dates the first explicit critical definition of it to 1935; *Irony*, p. 59.

and the reader, the observer. Distance is fundamental to the perception of irony, as Muecke's definition of irony makes clear, and the role of irony in controlling the distance between the reader and narrator, and the reader and other characters, as well as its effect on the reader-implied author relationship, will be examined in order to determine the reader's response to each novel.

CHAPTER II

MUERTES DE PERRO: THE SELF-CONSCIOUS NARRATOR

In *Muertes de perro* the reader follows a first-person narrator, Luis Pinedo, as he prepares to chronicle the downfall of his country's previous regime, headed by President Antón Bocanegra, and the rise of the latest strong men. The resulting manuscript is both personal narrative and chronicle, incorporating a self-critical running commentary, which reveals as much about its author as about his countrymen. Viewing characters and events as he does from alongside the narrator, the reader initially stands removed from the other characters, who must pass through the narrator's focus before reaching him. Yet the inclusion in Pinedo's narrative of other first-person presentations allows the reader to establish his own distance relationship from these re-narrated self-images. Further, the discrepancy between Pinedo's viewpoint on other characters and their self-presentations, despite Pinedo's control in excerpting and commenting, leads the reader to formulate his own distinct viewpoint toward the material provided by the narrator. This viewpoint coincides with that of the implied author and serves to distance the reader from the narrator, on whom he initially relies and with whom he continues to travel, by establishing a framework within which to view the narrator as well as his narrative.

Pinedo's tone in the opening chapters, which establish the epic situation prior to the inclusion of the first excerpts from documents and conversations, guides the reader in breaking away from his viewpoint. Pinedo's sarcasm and vituperation, his false humility and vainglory — in short, both his opinions and his rhetorical presentation — signal a viewpoint with which the reader, who has as yet encountered no basis for this tone, cannot identify, although Pinedo's physical limitations (he is confined to a wheelchair) do earn him a certain immediate degree of sympathy. In short, alongside his visible negative qualities, Pinedo does not display any positive attraction, apart from holding the information on which the reader is dependent. Thus while the reader acknowledges his debt to Pinedo for having prepared the manuscript, he does not view the manuscript from the same perspective as the narrator, but stands back at a point from which to encompass both Pinedo and his narrative.

Reading beyond the narrator's words and establishing himself on a plane outside the narration, the reader perceives an interpretation in the juxtaposition of thought, word and action which differs from that of the narrator who operates closer to the text. But the reader of fiction is not necessarily constrained to be in total agreement with this superior — by virtue of distance and comprehension — perspective; he may, according to Booth, reject its values. The norms which the implied author of *Muertes de perro* represents are strictly relativistic, in contrast to the prevailing imagery and the narrator's tone. Ayala has described the position of the implied author relative to the text, without of course terming it as such, as a function of the words themselves:

> En algún aspecto, me he limitado a repetir lo que magistralmente hiciera Galdós: dejar que las palabras traicionen los pensamientos de sus personajes y hasta delaten aquellos fondos de su conciencia que son arcanos para el propio sujeto. Pero, además, he pretendido por mi parte, al emplear las palabras y locuciones de uso común, apretarlas, estrujarlas y exprimirlas para extraer de ellas todo su posible contenido, de modo que signifiquen varias cosas a un tiempo, irradiando sentidos diversos y, en ocasiones, contradictorios. Es decir, que me he propuesto sacar todo el partido posible a la esencial ambigüedad del habla.[1]

In the sense that the reader does not rely on his evaluations, either of others or of himself, Pinedo can be characterized as an unreliable narrator. While he is not deliberately misleading — indeed he rather openly declares his biases and records his manipulations

---

[1] Ayala, "El fondo sociológico en mis novelas," p. 545.

of the texts in the name of historical truth — his conscious presentation of himself is quite naturally flawed; the degree to which the flaws result in deception is only manifest at the close of the narrative. In addition, the physical distance separating Pinedo from the other characters yields a gulf of misunderstanding. For example, his resentment against Tadeo Requena on this score is undeniable, if justifiable:

> ¡Doctorcito en Leyes, y sin tardanza! Durante cinco años tuve yo que rodar, con mis piernas inútiles, por las aulas, para poder llamarme abogado, mientras que ahora, éste... [873]

In such matters, Pinedo's unreliability results from his personal bias which forces the reader to formulate his own perspective on the characters. The reader must be an active participant in the novel's communication process, drawing from the words and actions of the narrator's text his own interpretation of the motivations and relationships which the historian, for lack of documentation as much as insight, proclaims himself unable to fathom. Indeed, Pinedo's method leaves much of the task of synthesizing to the reader. While his commentary introduces and concludes the selected passages from written and oral texts, he does not intrude upon their integrity and he frequently labels his conjectures as such. His commentary on the manuscript sources guides the reader in formulating his response:

> yo me pregunto si esta observación de Tadeo representa una crítica, si expresa rencor, o si rezuma admiración. No acierto con la respuesta, aunque me inclino a pensar que todos esos sentimientos pueden hallarse mezclados en su ánimo, sin que él mismo se diera completa cuenta. [899]

Perhaps Pinedo's vituperations against the invisible presence of "la crapulosa esfinge" [1014] Olóriz, his resentful antipathy toward Tadeo and his pervasive tone of superiority, as much as the absence of any identifiably positive characters in the narrative, lead the reader to adopt a more charitable view than Pinedo's, or perhaps it is in imitation of the chronicler's task, which Pinedo sets forth, that the reader is drawn away from adopting Pinedo's perspective.

Pinedo himself reiterates that judgments are relative, stressing the dimension of time in altering perspectives. Introducing the theme of the irretrievable past — *el bien perdido,* Pinedo illustrates this relativity of human judgment as regards the subject matter of his narrative, the Bocanegra regime:

> Muy mala, pésima era la situación de nuestro país bajo el gobierno de Bocanegra. Sin sus demagogias, no hubiéramos rodado hasta donde hoy nos vemos. Pero si, desde el hondón, volvemos la mirada hacia aquel tirano, su imagen se nos confunde ahora, casi, con la del bien perdido: tan relativas son las cosas de este mundo. [918]

Of Bocanegra himself Pinedo writes, underscoring the impact of distance on the narrator's perspective, "no sé ya si [el nombre de Bocanegra] deberá calificarse de infame, según pensábamos muchos, o más bien enaltecerlo y llorarlo como esperanza frustrada y malogrado remedio de la Patria." [861] This same theme is repeated in association with public opinion about the First Lady, as recorded with some irony by Pinedo: "Así, mucha gente que detestaba a doña Concha, la Presidenta, ha terminado por compadecer su triste suerte, y hasta por descubrirle algunas póstumas virtudes." [938] Although Pinedo does not signal the relativism resulting from the duality of his perspective on Tadeo Requena as such, the reader is alert to this effect of narrative distance. The temporal distance from which Pinedo narrates — the events he chronicles are already history with the single exception of the last chapter — thus constitutes his most valuable perspective. All the first-person narrators, by the very nature of the narrative act, narrate at a perceptible distance from the event recorded, a distance which in itself implies interpretation. But this distance is minimal, except in Pinedo's case and when Tadeo draws past events, such as his childhood and the establishment of his relationship with Doña Concha, into his diary. The dual temporal perspective inherent in the more distant relationship of the narrator-chronicler to his narrator-source, as well as in his personal reminiscences, allows Pinedo to record the effects of temporal distance in describing the current scene:

> estrangulaciones, y puñaladas, y fusilamientos, y horrores de todas clases, se encuentran a la orden del día, como si aun el último sentimiento humano hubiera desaparecido.

> Y en comparación, las querellas de ayer se nos antojan pequeñeces; pues lo que pasa ahora ha alterado las medidas antiguas, cambiando por completo los criterios que antes se tenían por válidos.... al lado de lo que hoy usurpa irrisoriamente el nombre de gobierno, el gobierno de Antón Bocanegra hubiera merecido parangonarse con el de Marco Aurelio: tan relativas son las cosas de esta vida. [937-38]

As narrator, Pinedo cannot achieve this same dual perspective on himself, even as the other narrators cannot, and this again becomes the task of the reader who can view the narrator's final projection of himself in terms of his opening self-presentation. Nevertheless, Pinedo is a self-conscious, if limited, narrator throughout, manipulating his projected image, perhaps nowhere as clearly as in the role he assigns himself in his recorded conversations with his Aunt Loreto.

Initially Pinedo impresses the reader with his narrative control, in part precisely as a result of his projected self-image. And yet the tone of his references to Olóriz — "este viejo Olóriz, lisiado ya y no menos impedido que yo, medio imbécil de senilidad" [858] — reveals from the start his deep-set antipathy, heightened by his continual references to the state of fear in which he lives, a fear which Pinedo's seemingly minor significance does not fully justify in the eyes of the reader. While the reader is thus unknowingly being prepared for Pinedo's ultimate loss of control, he is in no way led to anticipate this ending. The conversion of Pinedo from observer to actor and his concomitant defense of his actions, which definitively lift the narrative from the rough draft of a chronicle of the Bocanegra era to the narrative of human life against the backdrop of political turmoil, yields a last and larger perspective from which to view the entire narrative. The reader, his perspective on Pinedo suddenly enlarged, must rethink Pinedo's entire narration in terms of the closing pages, thus prolonging the reader's role beyond the confines of the novel. While initially the narrator is a secondary, if not tertiary, character, the ending of his narration makes clear that he is also a protagonist, the main character of his own document; the secondary characters whose lives he portrays for the reader serve to establish other perspectives from which to view his action. By the time the reader learns of Olóriz's addition to the long series of murder victims, he has formulated his response to the other characters. Thus when his evaluation of Pinedo is abruptly but not without preparation heightened, these evaluations form the parameters of his rethinking of Pinedo's character. As Bertil Romberg concludes in detailing the importance of the epic situation in *Doktor Faustus*: "the epic situation here is magnified and has a value of its own, beyond its normal function of creating the illusion of reality or producing tension and excitement." [2]

It remains to be pointed out that while the reader rejects Pinedo's self-image and therefore does not identify with him, this does not imply a total rejection of Pinedo since the narrative contains no truly positive or negative pole either to attract or repulse the reader; instead, the participant reader must establish his own position, independent of any within the text and yet adhering to the norms of the work itself. This leads him to a position of relativity from which each character is viewed as both guilty and innocent; in short, human. Only the idiot Ángelo is truly innocent, but his innocence hardly forms a standard of comparison from which to measure the other characters. Nevertheless, Tadeo Requena's concern for Ángelo, albeit tardy and shortlived, goes a long way towards redeeming him in a narrative in which no other character manifests that degree of concern for another, except María Elena in her notebook confession of her retrospective concern for her father. Brother and sister are furthermore the most sympathetic characters, in part because of their youth with its implicit innocence, in part because of the unfeeling manner in which they are disposed of after their father's death. Symbolically, it is only the wholly innocent Ángelo who manages to escape from society's constraints and the manipulations of others to live in complete independence and freedom. There is doubtless a reflection of Tadeo's life, prior to his being summoned by President Bocanegra, in Ángelo's street urchin existence.

Pinedo's narrative perspective is limited by his first-hand acquaintance with some of the characters involved and by his collection of first-person documents. His sources fall into three major categories:

---

[2] Romberg, p. 36.

1) written first-person documents — Tadeo Requena's diary,[3] the letter files of the Spanish Minister, and the papers of the Mother Superior of the convent of Santa Rosa, the latter containing the schoolgirl notebooks of María Elena Rosales;

2) reported conversations between Pinedo and a series of acquaintances, including the newspaperman Camarasa; the parish priest of San Cosme and chaplain of Santa Rosa, Don Antonio; Pinedo's Aunt Loreto; Pinedo's fellow boarder Sobrarbe; Pinedo's sometime employer and Loreto's uncle, Olóriz; as well as references to the variety of opinions collected by Pinedo from fellow frequenters of El Gran Café y Billares de la Aurora;

---

[3] Pinedo refers to the scattered pages of Tadeo Requena's manuscript as *memorias,* but they lack the distant and unified narrative perspective associated with the novelistic classification of fictional memoir. In contrast, Pinedo's own manuscript, which maintains its narrative distance from the plane of action except in the closing chapter, clearly exemplifies the fictional memoir.

Romberg divides the written epic situation into three fundamental types: fictitious memoir, diary novel and epistolary novel, describing the diary novel as follows:

> The diary novel gives the author the opportunity of letting the narrator and the reader come up against the action of the novel simultaneously, or at least experience its future happenings with the same degree of uncertainty. The fiction in a diary novel is both narrated and experienced gradually. The narrator's epic situation does not give him any all-embracing and definitive retrospective view over the events covered by his story, but only some short, concentrated, frequent backward glances.

pp. 35, 43. Although Tadeo's manuscript, and similarly José Lino Ruiz's manuscript in Part I of *El fondo del vaso,* do not technically conform to the diary format with its etymological implication of daily entries and hence a consistent narrative distance from the plane of action, the translation "diary" will be employed in both cases, in accordance with Romberg's distinction between epic situations. To refer to the personal record of one period of Tadeo Requena's life as his memoirs, even though it initially contains a retrospective description of his earlier years, does not adequately reflect the predominant narrative distance which ranges from immediate to one day or at most several weeks from the plane of action. By referring to his sporadic entries as constituting a diary, this narrative distance is underscored. But it must be remembered that neither Tadeo's nor José Lino's manuscript is formally recorded as a diary, consisting rather of loose sheets or notebooks which reflect the unpremeditated nature of each narrator's decision to keep a personal record. At least one previous critic has termed Tadeo Requena's manuscript a *diario;* Ricardo Gullón, "Francisco Ayala: *Muertes de perro,*" *La Torre,* 6, No. 24 (1958), 173-76.

3) reported conversations contained in the first-person sources — Tadeo's diary records conversations with Chino López, Luisito Rosales, Antón Bocanegra, the President's wife Doña Concha, Loreto, the Galician Luna, and various mediums; Loreto recounts conversations with Doña Concha, Tadeo and the warden of the prison where Doña Concha died.

In addition, both Pinedo and the Spanish Ambassador refer to newspaper reports — the Ambassador further mentions radio broadcasts — which offer additional perspectives. Pinedo specifies that in this first, rough draft of his chronicle he is purposefully omitting newspaper sources, "cuya colección queda ahí siempre como fuente de valor secundario al servicio del historiador." [956] Further, as regards more recent events, including those contemporary with the narrative present, which lie outside the scope of the present undertaking, Pinedo affirms:

> el historiador posee todos los datos para, llegada la oportunidad, organizarlos dentro de un relato congruente y claro, desde la tormentosa sesión del gabinete, espontáneamente reunido en Palacio al cundir la noticia del asesinato de Bocanegra, hasta el momento presente. [1008]

The gamut of perspectives from which the present chronicle draws runs on the one hand from the diplomatic dispatches of an Hispanophile, to the bluntly uncharitable and self-serving letters of a Mother Superior and the reports of her actions offered somewhat ingenuously by Don Antonio; on the other hand, there are the accounts by some of the principals in the political events and their confidants. In all cases, every word reaches the reader from an identified, first-person perspective.

Pinedo considers the text he is preparing as merely a preliminary exercise, as he reiterates throughout. The chronicle which he proposes as an admonition to his countrymen will follow, "tan pronto como remita la ola de violencias, desmanes, asesinatos, robos, incendios y demás tropelías que afligen al país desde la muerte del Presidente Bocanegra." [861] In his position as self-conscious narrator, Pinedo records for himself the difference between the projected and the actual text, revealing that the mnemonic structure and spontaneity of the present would be subordinated to an imposed, chronological framework in the final version, thus further distancing Pinedo from the text through the heightened degree of control:

> Cuando, con más sosiego y en condiciones más normales, pueda yo redactar el texto definitivo de mi libro, habré de vigilarme y tener mucho cuidado de presentar los acontecimientos, no revueltos, como ahora, sino en su debido orden cronológico, de modo que aparezcan bien inteligibles y ostenten el decoro formal exigido en un relato histórico. Después de todo, no importa: estos papeles no son sino un ejercicio,... o a lo sumo recolección de materiales, borrador y anotación de detalles para no olvidarme luego de lo que se me ocurre y debo retener. [956]

At the core of Pinedo's documentation lies Tadeo Requena's diary, "la pieza maestra en la serie de documentos que estoy reuniendo y que me propongo extractar aquí como base de mi futuro libro." [865] Pinedo initially intends to reproduce only those passages from his source material which bear directly on the course of the regime, but it soon becomes evident, including to Pinedo himself, that it is Tadeo Requena, as reflected in "la multitud de pormenores triviales o accesorios, sólo relacionados con el autor mismo y sus preocupaciones" [865], who occupies the center of the manuscript. The result of this shift in focus from the events themselves to Tadeo's self-revelatory perspective is to:

> poner de relieve el ambiente de obsecuencia, servilismo y grotesco envilecimiento a que nos había conducido el régimen de Antón Bocanegra, al mismo tiempo que se perfila el retrato moral del tirano y también, de rechazo, el de este secretario que había de ser su asesino. [915]

The verbalization of Pinedo's awareness of the discrepancy between intent and result underscores his self-consciousness as narrator and further serves to forestall any possible reader dissatisfaction with his narrative construction. Pinedo's self-consciousness concerning the narrative process and his reiterated resolution to improve upon the existing text in the final draft continually turn aside potential reader criticism of it.

On the other hand, Pinedo unknowingly reveals to the reader the effect that direct contact with the full implications of the events he so distantly narrates produces on him. His literary task provides an escape from the atmosphere of terror in which he lives, as he admits, and yet too close contact with his documents produces the same sensations of revulsion in him:

> Me refugio yo y meto la cabeza entre mis papeles por no pensar en el peligro que acecha; pero, de pronto, cuando más distraído estoy, me entra el dichoso vértigo, siento una especie de mareo y náusea, empieza a darme todo vueltas alrededor, y es como si despertara de improviso a la cruda realidad. [937]

Indeed, this "awakening" foreshadows his real awakening at the narrative's end, preparing the reader for his response on that occasion. When his Aunt Loreto produces an old photograph of Antón Bocanegra and his wife Concha in their youth, the same sensation of nausea sweeps over Pinedo, who on this occasion does not propose a hypothetical explanation as earlier: "Sentí una cosa rara, especie de náusea, o vértigo, no sé." [952] The association with the earlier incident is nevertheless clear to the reader. Thus the narrative distance is graphically impressed upon the reader, who identifies the source of Pinedo's physical discomfort as the absence of his accustomed distant perspective.

Despite Pinedo's stated objective of leaving a "true historical account," Pinedo recognizes, as is obvious from the importance he places on first-hand accounts, that the truth arises from the juxtaposition of individual perspectives, and that the total picture is therefore an unattainable goal. Since Doña Concha died before Pinedo commenced his chronicle, her perspective is unattainable, except as recorded by Tadeo and Loreto. Although Doña Concha's role is transparent from the entries in Tadeo's diary, neither he, nor the seemingly superficial Loreto, nor Pinedo draws the obvious conclusion; this role is reserved for the reader. Like Doña Concha, although through different circumstances, Pancho Cortina, momentarily the most likely successor to Bocanegra and now incomunicado since his symbolic headlong descent down the palace stairs after avenging Bocanegra's death, is not available to add his perspective. Numerous incidents — Doña Concha's relationship with Cortina, for example, and his role in Bocanegra's death — are raised and never detailed for lack of these perspectives. As Pinedo acknowledges, somewhat facetiously since the degree to which the decision to speak up lies within Cortina's power is highly questionable, "ahí está todavía Pancho Cortina que, si le diera la gana, podría ilustrar hasta el menor detalle de los muchos que faltan." [1003]

In recognizing that the complete gamut of perspectives is inaccessible to him, Pinedo asserts that "los cuentos de la realidad quedan descabalados siempre." [1003] (In contrast, Tadeo contends in the last lines he writes that his purpose in leaving the record of his participation in Bocanegra's death is so that "el cuento no quede descabalado." [1003]) Pinedo's view of reality as expressed in his role as narrator coincides with Ortega's observations on the multiplicity of perspectives which constitute reality:

> Resulta, pues, que una misma realidad se quiebra en muchas realidades divergentes cuando es mirada desde puntos de vista distintos. Y nos ocurre preguntarnos: ¿cuál de esas múltiples realidades es la verdadera, la auténtica? Cualquiera decisión que tomemos será arbitraria. Nuestra preferencia por una u otra sólo puede fundarse en el capricho. Todas esas realidades son equivalentes, cada una la auténtica para su congruo punto de vista. Lo único que podemos hacer es clasificar estos puntos de vista y elegir entre ellos el que prácticamente parezca más normal o más espontáneo. Así llegaremos a una noción nada absoluta, pero, al menos, práctica y normativa de realidad.[4]

In a sense Pinedo is doing the reader's work for him in identifying the gaps in the completed fabric of his history and in pointing to the inaccessibility, symbolized by Doña Concha's death and Cortina's confinement to the hospital of the military prison, of the total picture. In contrast to the more traditional closed form, the open-ended nature of Pinedo's narrative leads the reader to be more concerned with the individual's perception both of himself and of others than with events. The perspectivistic structure de-emphasizes action, by focusing on point of view.

A prime example of the multiplicity of perspectives documented by Pinedo is the reader's access to Luisito Rosales, whom Pinedo, Tadeo Requena, the Mother Superior, Rosales' sister-in-law, his daughter María Elena and the Ambassador all comment upon, while

---

[4] Ortega y Gasset, III, p. 360.

the further perspectives of Doña Concha and Loreto reach the reader indirectly. Yet the image of Luisito Rosales is never firmly fixed in the reader's mind, since he is viewed so differently by so many; but a great deal of sympathy is generated by virtue of these contradictory and generally harsh judgments. First Tadeo's ambivalent attitude, signaled by Pinedo, not to mention his intentional cruelty towards Rosales, and later María Elena's sympathetic retrospective view of her adversary relationship with her father direct the reader's sympathetic tendencies.

In contrast to the multiple perspectives from which Luisito Rosales and other characters are viewed, Pinedo projects himself to the reader only directly, with the exception of a few re-narrated comments. This fact serves to strengthen the reader's acceptance of Pinedo's stated distance from the lives of the other characters, as well as requiring the reader to evaluate Pinedo by comparing his words and his actions and to infer his personality from his comments concerning others. From the opening lines of this preliminary draft of his chronicle Luis Pinedo — "el insignificante Pinedito" [858] in the eyes of others, as Pinedo himself records — insists upon both the importance of his position as a witness to the political era he is about to document and the disassociation from the events themselves with which his seeming insignificance and limited mobility provide him. He vaunts his privileged position, limited only by his powers of observation, his restricted mobility and his access to documents:

> Pocas son las cosas que escapan a mi observación en esta desconocida Atenas del trópico americano. Reducido por mi enfermedad al mero papel de espectador, desde mi butaca veo, percibo y capto lo que a otros, a casi todos, pasa inadvertido. Son las compensaciones que la perspectiva del sillón de ruedas ofrece al tullido. [864]

At the same time that Pinedo dwells on the impression of impotency which his confinement to a wheelchair causes, he projects a more vital self-image by underscoring the distance between appearance and potential for action. Foreshadowing the action which brings his narrative to a close, Pinedo asserts:

> Cierto es, lo sé bien, que mi condición no constituiría impedimento mayor para quien gustase de participar en las luchas de su tiempo. [858]

In projecting himself as a privileged but non-participatory witness separated not only by virtue of physical disability but by social and moral superiority from the "grotesca danza de la muerte" dominating the contemporary scene, Pinedo establishes an immediate distance between himself and the figures who enter into his narrative. While cherishing the certainty of achieving lasting fame in the judgment of history for having salvaged the documents from which his manuscript is built, a fame not inconsistent with his sense of personal worth, Pinedo simultaneously humbly disclaims any virtue in his undertaking. This humility is, however, expressed in purely rhetorical terms. He also renounces the image of a participant, a seemingly gratuitous renunciation at this point despite his assertions to the contrary. By the end of the first chapter the tone of humility is largely overshadowed by Pinedo's sense of the historical importance of his mission. The attraction which the role of sole guardian of the "true" history of the Bocanegra era holds out to him is clear:

> No disimularé que me ilusiona la perspectiva de ser yo mismo, si es que arribamos a buen puerto, el arquitecto de esa obra grandiosa. Es una tarea digna; vale la pena, y presiento que me está reservada. [859]

History itself has prepared Pinedo to fulfill the mission of chronicler:

> Acaricio, pues, la esperanza de que me esté reservada a mí, como descendiente que soy de una ilustre estirpe de letrados, gala y prestigio de esta tierra en tiempos menos infelices, la alta misión de impartir esa justicia histórica en un libro que, al mismo tiempo, sirva de admonición a las generaciones venideras y de permanente guía a este pueblo degenerado que alguna vez deberá recuperar su antigua dignidad, humillada hoy por nuestras propias culpas, pero no definitivamente perdida. [860-61]

Earlier this "ilustre estirpe de letrados" has been referred to by Pinedo as "una familia de escribas" [858], implying a less than aristocratic family heritage. The present degenerated, destitute state of the family is symbolized by Pinedo's physical self; in a tradition familiar to Spanish literature, Pinedo has become a parasite on society. But Pinedo sees his position as one of moral superiority to the reigning chaos. He projects himself as a savior come to redeem an erring but not yet damned people by confronting them with the record of their iniquities. When Pinedo takes up this role again in the closing lines of his narrative, it is in very different circumstances.

From the opening chapter it is evident that Pinedo protests too much in attempting to convey a convincingly equanimous image of himself. At the same time he almost proudly inserts comments which reveal the image he projects to others. Bocanegra, commenting on an article written by Pinedo, opines that "sólo un tipo como [Pinedo], amargado por su desgracia, podía destilar tanta hiel en unas cuantas líneas." [917] As the active but unobserved collector and guardian of documents, his handicap becomes his protective cover, and Pinedo vaunts the cleverness with which he manipulates the image of himself as incapacitated. As though to confirm his mission, documentation literally falls into his lap.

Pinedo's immediate objective as he writes is limited:

> Por lo pronto, ganaré tiempo aplicándome a la labor preparatoria de juntar y ordenar los materiales, allegar las fuentes dispersas, y trazar algún que otro comentario, aclaración o glosa que concierte y relacione entre sí los acontecimientos, depure los hechos y establezca el verdadero alcance y el cabal sentido de cada suceso. De esta manera, calmo mi ansiedad, lleno las horas y, en el caso en que la suerte no me acompañe hasta el final o me fallen las fuerzas, quedará siempre ahí un mamotreto crudo y un tanto caótico, sí, pero de cualquier modo útil; más diré, indispensable. [859]

By the very nature of the hypothetical circumstances he alludes to, the text is potentially definitive. From the first he reveals the insecurity of life under the new regime and the instability of the too observant chronicler in a suspicious and retributive society. The ominous note first sounds in his opening paragraph, preparing the way for the events which bring the narrative to a close:

> Si mi invalidez sigue valiéndome, si acaso no se le ocurre todavía a algún mala sangre divertirse a costa de este pobre tullido y meterme de un empujón en la grotesca danza de la muerte, es muy probable que lleguemos al final, y pueda contarlo... Porque esto ha de tener un final; y será menester que alguien lo cuente. [857]

Here Pinedo points the way to the inclusion in his narrative of a future which is as yet as unknown to him as to the reader and for which, therefore, he cannot knowingly prepare the reader. Even at the close of the narrative, the reader does not know how it has reached him, yet clearly some of what Pinedo feared must have come about to have brought this preliminary draft into circulation. The final chapter, of course, suggests the direction events have taken, but only the inclusion of an editor or other similar device could provide this information.

As defined in the first chapter of this study, every written text represents an act of communication with an implied reader as recipient of its message. Given Pinedo's conception of his narrative, the question arises as to whether he consciously takes the potential reader into account, for the distinction must be maintained between consciously employed narrative devices and such unconscious narrative devices as foreshadowing and prefiguration which only the reader identifies, attributing them to the hand of the implied author. The projected definitive version of the text is envisioned by Pinedo as serving a specific function in chronicling the political and moral corruption; hence the reader would be consciously in Pinedo's mind as he directed his "admonition" and "guide" to him. But even as he prepares this first draft, Pinedo at times consciously, at times only rhetorically or unconsciously, structures his presentation to elicit a desired response from an implied reader. Despite his early references to circumstances in which he might lose control over his manuscript, references which serve to uphold the fact of the reader's present access to the text, at various later points Pinedo specifically denies that his text will be read by others than himself. But even these statements do not contradict the fact that parts of the narrative are consciously directed by Pinedo to an audience.

Of the rhetorical devices, which by their very nature imply a recipient, the first appears early in the opening chapter as Pinedo reveals his self-consciousness as narrator with the apology, "perdónese la digresión." [860] After introducing an entry from Tadeo Requena's diary, Pinedo withdraws from his role as narrator with the concluding phrase, "En fin, júzguese por sus propias palabras, que yo quiero limitarme a copiar." [959] In further recognition of the reader's role, Pinedo initiates his commentary of María Elena's written confession with the acknowledgement, "como podrá advertir en seguida el avisado y discreto lector." [981] While Pinedo may be employing these rhetorical appeals to the reader unwittingly, he nevertheless displays a consciousness of the reader's response to his narration.

References to the techniques of detective fiction, mentioned twice by Pinedo, introduce the relationship between his text and the detective genre. Although the events themselves would qualify for detective fiction treatment, as Pinedo seems to acknowledge, he does not handle them in this way. Rather, he focuses on the individual awareness and response, not on the manner in which events occurred nor on providing an acceptable explanation for each detail. The multiple perspectives serve to illuminate personalities to a larger degree than actions. While writing from the vantage point of his completed collection of documents, Pinedo does not assume an omniscient viewpoint but rather guides the reader in retracing his own access to an increasingly fuller perspective through the accumulation of additional points of view. However, on stated occasions he alters this order, as when he inserts Loreto's perspective on Bocanegra's murder, gleaned from Pinedo's conversation with her, prior to copying Tadeo's account into his narrative. Pinedo intentionally toys with both the unsuspecting Loreto and the alerted reader by failing to clarify her confused perception of these events:

> Las puntuales memorias de Tadeo me habían proporcionado la clave de ese misterio; yo había leído por adelantado el desenlace en las últimas páginas de la novela y, como un detective que se reserva ciertos datos para sorprender al lector, estaba en condiciones de desenredar la trama.... Mas yo no tenía interés alguno en ofrecerle la solución a Loreto. [946-47]

His references to Loreto being merely a ploy, Pinedo is clearly announcing to the reader the technique in which he is engaging.

Returning to the "mystery" later, after holding the reader in suspense for several chapters, Pinedo reminds the reader of his superior knowledge withheld from Loreto:

> Durante mi conversación con tía Loreto, de la que adelanté ya alguna noticia, hubo de quedar flotando en el aire, como quizá se recuerde, un pequeño problema de novela detectivesca, cuya clave por rara ventura poseo. [999]

Here Pinedo is, of course, making obvious use of understatement, since the "small problem" holds the key to the major events of his history and since Tadeo's diary contains this key. Clearly aware of the effect on the waiting reader, Pinedo has withheld Tadeo's perspective, which supplements and in some respects supplants Loreto's, until he has copied the preceding portions of the diary. The parallel with techniques of detective fiction is clear, and Pinedo returns to the comparison in clarifying his own narrative technique:

> Si me propusiera yo escribir esa novela de misterio desplegaría toda una serie de hipótesis ingeniosas, como posibles soluciones alternativas, antes de resolverme a ofrecer la verdadera a la voracidad del curioso lector; pero como no se trata aquí de novelas más o menos entretenidas, sino de establecer los hechos históricos, debo apresurarme a informarlo, mediante documentos fidedignos, escuetamente, de lo que en verdad aconteció. [999-1000]

Through manipulating the release of information, the narrator can mislead the dependent reader and, despite his disclaimer, Pinedo has altered the reader's perspective by not recording all the information in the sequence in which he received it. Nevertheless, his references to fiction do have the effect of establishing the distinction between detective novels and Pinedo's "true" narrative and of reinforcing the credibility of the latter by this reference. The effects of withholding the key information is deliberate in bringing Tadeo Requena's diary to its conclusion in the closing chapters of Pinedo's manuscript, despite the fact that it was the first document he obtained. Unaware of his approaching fate, Pinedo can only be intending to draw the reader along as far as possible before offering the *pièce de resistence,* in the suspense-filled tradition of the detective novel. The reader must attribute the capricious chronology to

Pinedo, while recognizing that the effect it produces in presenting the parallel between Tadeo Requena's murder of Bocanegra and Pinedo's murder of Olóriz in close succession lies outside his control. Pinedo further displays this manipulation of chronology in waiting until he has completed extracting information from the diary to explain how it reached him; the explanation is implicitly directed at excusing this authorial privilege to the reader. An earlier disclosure would have placed the circumstances of Tadeo's death before Tadeo's diary entries and before Loreto's recollections of the events of that night. Pinedo's own perspective as a distant observer whose involvement came only the morning following Tadeo's death thus reaches the reader last. As a historian Pinedo reconstructs these events in the sequence in which they occurred, building on the converging perspectives at his disposal. This departure from his earlier self-described chaotic construction elicits the reference to the tightly controlled structure of detective fiction.

The reader's credulousness is most sharply called to account in accepting the fact that he holds Pinedo's preliminary draft in his hands, the manner in which documentation reaches Pinedo, the fact that Tadeo Requena keeps a highly literate personal record, and the fact that María Elena engages in a lengthy and rhetorical outpouring of emotions following her father's suicide and her own uncontested rape. As has been pointed out in reference to the text which the reader is reading, Pinedo attempts to meet and dispel potential reader disbelief. Romberg recognizes that a narrator's point of view must be credible "not only with regard to time and space but also to the narrator's mental capacity." The question to be asked is, "Is his intellectual equipment capable of the exposition?"[5] Pinedo strives to account for both the secondary narrators' propensity to write and the manner in which they write, and furthermore to convince the reader that they have indeed written by references to the visual appearance of their manuscripts. (In the case of María Elena's notebooks, these observations are contained in the Mother Superior's letter to the aunt.) Such is the function of the reference to Tadeo Requena's misspellings — ironically a criticism which Tadeo himself makes of the poetry of the native poet laureate Camilo Zapato so that a hierarchy of literary snobbery

---

[5] Romberg, p. 94.

is evident — while the general neatness of the drafts of the Mother Superior's letter from her correspondence file testifies to the haste and surety with which the final draft followed the preliminary one.

On another level reader preparation occurs within the narrator's text but without the reader's awareness of the future importance of the information. When Pinedo reveals his access to Olóriz and Olóriz's nocturnal habits, neither he nor the reader can be aware of the ominous import of his boast that his low profile, "me permite estar cerca de él, verlo a cualquier hora del día o de la noche, hablarle." [940] Nor is Tadeo Requena aware of the manner in which Doña Concha will take advantage of his role as "guardián y sumiller" [906] of Bocanegra's special stock of whiskey. Pinedo draws the reader's attention to the prefigurative force of this passage, commenting about Tadeo's diary:

> Casi siempre, los datos que nos ofrece el secretario encierran algo de curioso, aunque no siempre resulten trascendentales, ni siquiera importantes en sí mismos. Hay veces en que su importancia se relaciona con hechos posteriores a la ocasión, o que son consecuencia de algo cuyo papel no hubiera podido barruntarse entonces, y que se ilumina retrospectivamente. [905-6]

Here Pinedo displays his self-consciousness not only as narrator but as a reader, and in so doing alerts the reader of his narrative to his role.

When Tadeo Requena's diary comes to an abrupt end with a last separate sheet written after he has shot President Bocanegra, the epic situation leads Pinedo to exclaim, "¡bajo tales circunstancias y en aquellos momentos: singular manía!" [1002] Immediately following this, however, Pinedo recognizes that this last page is no longer so much a personal record as Tadeo's attempt to communicate his perspective on Bocanegra's death to a potential reader in the now foreseeable event of his own death or incapacitation. Pinedo then rectifies his earlier judgment and in so doing reveals how he has again manipulated the reader's response with this precipitous outburst, which doubtless reproduces his own initial response to the entry. At the same time, any possible reader disinclination to accept the verisimilitud of Tadeo's last page is being channelled into the mainstream of Pinedo's argument and controverted:

> No, no era manía, ni tampoco una pueril preocupación literaria, que, en la ocasión, hubiera resultado demasiado inconcebible; sino que el joven Requena, sospechándose cogido en una trampa de la que tal vez su instinto le había prevenido aunque en vano, quiso, a todo evento, dejar esas líneas donde constan de su puño y letra los hechos decisivos, con lo cual, si su aprensión resultaba cierta, podrían servir de prueba acusadora contra su cómplice, y vengarlo. La aparición oportuna de esos papeles explotaría como una bomba llegado el momento. [1002]

This reconstruction of Tadeo's motivation to write parallels Tadeo's earlier confession that "esa mujer está pudiendo conmigo," and his decision at that point to initiate a record of their relationship in the awareness of its potential value in protecting him against her machinations: "ahora necesito ponerlo en negro sobre blanco, para cualquier eventualidad." [985] The ironic fact that Tadeo's revelations never reach the public until Pinedo's own manuscript somehow does is compounded by the irony that this manuscript in its present state is not intended to reach beyond Pinedo himself. Pinedo justifies his withholding of these pages from circulation by declaring, "la Historia misma lo ha vengado ya sin necesidad de ellos" [1002]; that is, to Pinedo's mind the death of Tadeo's accomplice and double traitor Doña Concha has avenged his own. But Tadeo's concern, as his final sentences affirm, is that the "true" circumstances, from his perspective, be made public, exonerating him to some extent:

> dejo en este papel noticia de lo sucedido, cosa de que el cuento no quede descabalado. Mi disparo, después de todo, no ha hecho más que precipitar la muerte que ya Bocanegra tenía dentro del cuerpo; quizá, ahorrarle sufrimientos; despenarlo. [1003]

Thus Tadeo attempts to justify the shooting of Bocanegra, absolving himself from any guilt in this crime, on the grounds that Bocanegra was already dying of poison, and ignoring the fact that he himself administered the poison under Doña Concha's tutelage. Indeed, Tadeo seeks to turn the murder into an act of mercy. The importance of considering Tadeo's last testament and disclaimer of guilt, directed to the public as much as to justifying himself in his own eyes, lies in its parallel with passages from Pinedo's own narrative.

Admitting to rumors concerning the death of his acquaintance, the newspaperman Camarasa, whose forth-rightness brought only fear to Pinedo, the latter complains:

> no falta quien haya echado a rodar la especie de que he sido yo también quien denunció a Camarasa, dando lugar a que lo asesinaran. Prefiero, por lo tanto, agarrar al toro por los cuernos y dejar esclarecidas las cosas de una vez por todas; y que cada cual cargue con la responsabilidad que le corresponda. [917]

Seemingly, Pinedo is offering to put on record — here implying once again that his manuscript is directed at a reading public — the truth concerning this rumor, implicitly to clear his name in the eyes of his countrymen. However, the wily Pinedo doubles back, leaving the matter of Camarasa's death dangling unanswered, ironically shirking the dictum of his strongly-worded closing on responsibility which sets the stage for a distribution of charges. Instead, Pinedo admits only to having written a certain anonymous article, attacking an apparently rather naively absurd piece by Camarasa, an action Pinedo strongly defends in the narrative present in contrast to the protective mask of anonymity he wore at the time he wrote this "virulencia vitriólica" [916], as he proudly terms it now. Thus in a sense by verbally "murdering" Camarasa, Pinedo is at least symbolically implicated in his death. But the context of Pinedo's declaration, when he has set the reader up to expect a denial, makes this even clearer.

Pinedo first raises the question of the authorship of the anonymous attack, announcing, "Y aquí, en este punto, es donde me interesa a mí aclarar las cosas." [916] Juxtaposed to this firm tone, Pinedo's revelation that Tadeo and others at the Presidential palace attributed the article to him and his seemingly brave stand that "de poco valdría que yo quisiera suprimir ahora el pasaje correspondiente [al artículo] en las memorias" [916], would appear to mean that he is denying the authorship. Instead, at this point, following the introduction of the second accusation, Pinedo turns back around to proudly declare his authorship. The circumstances of Camarasa's death are never detailed, nor is the exact nature of

Pinedo's employment by Olóriz which may provide the link with it. Whereas the reader anticipates a denial from Pinedo on both charges, he receives a firmly asserted confirmation of the first and only an eventual rhetorical disassociation from the second. By the very momentum built up in Pinedo's description of the circumstances surrounding the publication of the article, and the juxtaposition of the two charges, the reader associates the two, as Pinedo seemingly intends, thus anticipating Pinedo's confirmation of the second charge as well as the first. Eventually, Pinedo's train of association leads him back to the subject of Camarasa's death, from which he recoils with the renunciation:

> ¿qué culpa voy a tener yo, ni por qué regla de tres me han de meter a mí en esto? Si vamos a hilar delgado, todos tenemos la culpa de todo cuanto pasa en el mundo, y a todos por fas o por nefas, nos incumbe alguna responsabilidad. Sería chistoso que ahora resultara yo ... [918]

This mock horror provides only an implicit denial, while the assertion about responsibility constitutes a denial of the Christian concept that every man is his brother's keeper, in contrast to the earlier imagery of the sacred mission which Pinedo is destined to carry out. Pinedo's very tone alienates rather than convinces the reader; indeed, Pinedo seems to be bluffing. But only after finishing the novel, after Pinedo has reiterated his involvement in Olóriz's department of "Servicios especiales y reservados," does the reader really feel Pinedo capable of playing a role in Camarasa's death.

Pinedo's implicit defense of his actions in recording the ebb and flow of his ties with his Aunt Loreto and his present employer Olóriz, following the tides of political fortune, passes this oscillation off as initially unpremeditated and purely instinctual [919], as well as necessary for a man in his straitened circumstances. Riding the crest of Loreto's influence as Doña Concha's confidante, Pinedo draws closer to Olóriz's purse strings, observing ominously that, "quién maneja una asignación bajo la rúbrica de *Servicios especiales y reservados,* sabido es cuánto puede hacer discrecionalmente." [920] Then drawing back from this insinuated pride in power, Pinedo adopts a defensive, pathetic tone as he presents his situation to the judgment of the implied reader: "Por lo que a mí concierne, ¿qué remedio me quedaba, tampoco?; tenía que seguir viviendo, ¿no?" [920] Not surprisingly for the reader, Pinedo's defense is based on personal expediency. Following as it does his attempted disassociation from the responsibility for the actions of others and his only implicit denial of a role in Camarasa's death, his further self-justification here strikes the reader as additional evidence of his weakness and opportunism. Ironically, he can fault Tadeo for his "dudosas moralidades" [889] in dismissing the death of Lucas Rosales.

When first discussing Camarasa's death, after recording his conversation on the state of the regime with the outspoken newspaperman, Pinedo asserts:

> La verdad es que no podía tener otro final que el que ha tenido, por muy lamentable que ello sea. Cada cual es el autor de su propia suerte; cada uno es el primer y principal responsable de lo que venga a sucederle. No se puede ser impunemente tan desatentado como él era... [877]

Pinedo's fear at hearing Camarasa's openly expressed judgments finds justification in Camarasa's fate; self-preservation, as Pinedo only half admits above, is his game. The dictum that an individual seals his own fate satisfies Pinedo when applied to Camarasa; ironically, Pinedo is moving blindly towards his own. Without specifying their nature, Pinedo makes oblique reference to certain services he has performed for Olóriz — "este inmundo carcamal" [1012] — in exchange for much-needed income: "con alguna periodicidad había debido hacerme abonos, por este o aquel concepto, de los fondos a su cargo." [919] The implications are tremendous, given Pinedo's insistence from the first pages of his manuscript, on Olóriz's power and methods of operation; rhetorically he asserts:

> ¿No es él quien decreta muertes bajo pretexto de pública salvación, quien ordena interrogatorios y dispone torturas, y maneja, en suma, desde su rincón, los hilos todos de los títeres? Él es, aunque mentira parezca. [858]

Pinedo's own indiscretion in talking of Olóriz with his Aunt Loreto, at a moment when he is feeling especially confident about the security of his position under Olóriz's command, immediately precedes Olóriz's questioning of him concerning his interest in the details of recent political events. Thus Pinedo moves along the same path he so sharply visualized in Camarasa's case.

Like Tadeo's diary, Pinedo's manuscript climaxes in murder, with the difference that Pinedo's murder of Olóriz cannot be explicitly prepared for in the opening pages of the manuscript. However, in lamenting the "criminal alliance" formed between Tadeo and Doña Concha, Pinedo specifically includes himself among those who were to suffer its consequences [928], when ironically he cannot know how far the train of events it set in motion will eventually carry him. In both Pinedo's and Tadeo's manuscripts the narrative distance becomes minimal in the closing pages and the tone, intimate. Pinedo still seems to direct his justification at an implicit reader, as does Tadeo more explicitly, but the manner is less detached and reasoned; his emotions raised to their highest pitch, Pinedo exudes self-confidence and exults in his cleverness. His early assertion to the reader that, although confined to a wheelchair, his capacity for action is not diminished has been realized. In contrast to his earlier self-confidence, in the pages immediately preceding his last, fateful conversation with Olóriz, Pinedo engages in a renewed defense of his policy of currying the favor of the all-powerful presence behind the current triumvirate:

> En estas condiciones, ¿cómo no comprender, y perdonar — pues la necesidad carece de ley —, que cada cual, si no encuentra modo mejor de proteger su pellejo, trate de disimularse entre la jauría, en evitación de que, un día u otro, a falta de más apetecibles piezas...? [1014]

Ironically, Pinedo's very next entry, juxtaposed to this restatement of his fear, laments his having indeed become Olóriz's latest intended victim. As with Camarasa, he has based his self-defense on expediency, on the every-man-for-himself philosophy, but his intended protector has become his potential destroyer. This structural juxtaposition prepares the reader for Pinedo's decision to murder Olóriz, even as his insistence from the very start on the reigning atmosphere of fear has set the stage for his emotional response to Olóriz. First surprise and fear, then humiliation, anger and finally a mood of cold calculation sweep over Pinedo. The parallel with Tadeo as he waited for the news of Bocanegra's death to spread is clear to Pinedo as well as to the reader who, if he has not drawn the comparison for himself, has it clearly outlined for him:

> He regresado a casa con la muerte en el cuerpo; se comprenderá. Y ahora, después de garrapatear estas líneas (¡ya estoy como el Tadeo Requena!, pero es que, no siendo fumador, sólo el escribir me ayuda a tranquilizar los nervios). [1016]

The second and closing section of Pinedo's manuscript follows his murder of Olóriz and, like Tadeo's closing page, represents both self-justification and a call for comprehension. To Pinedo his action is heroic, but his narrative offers little corroboration that his assertions concerning Olóriz's power are correct. Truly now a protagonist, a wielder of the sword not the pen, another Tadeo Requena, Pinedo has revealed himself to be all that he said he was not. He has joined the ranks of those he originally characterized condescendingly: "Ellos pugnan, ellos luchan, ellos se desgarran, ellos se arrancan la vida y, movidos por oleadas de ciega pasión, actúan como protagonistas." [858] As when he wrote the attack on Camarasa, he seems to delight that no one will know "cuál es el nombre del ciudadano benemérito a quién algún día deberá levantar una estatua la Nación, reconocida." [1017] In insanely exhilarated tones, Pinedo sees the fulfillment of his desire for earthly fame as a national hero, the savior of his people. To Tadeo the shooting of Bocanegra could even be construed as a blessing in disguise, a sort of euthanasia; Pinedo fantasizes having performed a service to the entire nation, envisioning as well that nation's gratitude to him once it has sought his identity out. But even as Tadeo chooses to ignore that he poisoned Bocanegra in submitting his final defense, Pinedo dismisses the element of crime; nevertheless, Pinedo's closing lines are by far the less rational.

The reader's role is duplicated in these two documents; he is the recipient of a last confession, entrusted with the defendants' line of defense. At this point, Pinedo's perspective becomes for him the only true perspective, in ironic defiance of the historian's task as he elaborated it throughout the manuscript. Interestingly, Pinedo offered no comment on Tadeo's final words, and now the judgment of Pinedo's closing lines lies entirely in the reader's hands as well. As the reader has come to realize throughout the narrative, Pinedo's perspective does not suffice; reading beneath the surface, in the contrast of word and action and in the parallel offered by Tadeo Requena's diary, the reader has established his own, all-encompassing perspective from which to view narrator and narrative.

After discovering in Tadeo Requena's diary a surprisingly articulate, observant and imperturbable individual, unimagined previously by Pinedo, the historian in Pinedo laments:

> Ahora el hombre ya no existe: lástima no haber reparado más en él y haberlo observado mejor, cuando vivía. Pero ¡cualquiera adivina! ... [890]

The same sentiment would serve as Pinedo's epitaph as well. Pinedo's basic antipathy toward Tadeo stems from the latter's instant transformation from a rural unknown to Presidential secretary. He focuses on Tadeo's pride in attacking him:

> la inmensa vanidad que le rezumaba por todos los poros de la piel, sólo contenida, restañada y sofrenada de cuando en cuando por la no menor insultante soberbia que le era connatural y que producía en él una extraña combinación de inseguridad y aplomo. [873]

The description strongly reflects Pinedo's character as well. At the same time, Pinedo begrudgingly recognizes the importance of Tadeo's role in his chronicle of the Bocanegra regime:

> el oscuro secretario a quien su acto homicida, y sólo su acto homicida, ha colocado luego en el centro de los acontecimientos históricos. [873]

Pinedo's own case is identical, although he cannot know it; nor can the reader on the first reading, but the prefigurative force of the passage stands. Indeed Pinedo, by virtue of murdering Olóriz, becomes the pivotal character of his own narrative, as Tadeo and the other narrators are of theirs. Whereas Pinedo purports to focus his chronicle on Antón Bocanegra, in reality Tadeo Requena fills the center of the screen as a result of his first-person account; in turn, with the close of Pinedo's manuscript, Pinedo himself moves to stage center, the primary subject of his own narrative, while Tadeo Requena is seen as a parallelistic figure, one step removed from the narrative focus.

To the reader, Pinedo's comments on Tadeo often apply to himself as well. Early in the narrative, on the basis of discovering in Tadeo the same inclination to record life, Pinedo raises the unsettling question of their possible similarity despite his unyielding judgment of Tadeo as "despreciable en definitiva":

> ¿De modo que este sujeto gris...; quiero decir que, en el fondo, era uno como yo, un animal de mi especie, un congénere mío? [864]

The narrative distance allows this dual perspective on Tadeo, as Pinedo's deep-set antipathy comes up against their common responses through his reading, in the narrative present, of Tadeo's diary. Tadeo's essentially distant perspective on people and events evokes criticism from Pinedo, who himself is more consistently distant than the more self-preoccupied Tadeo. Expressing his revulsion at this distancing, Pinedo characterizes the hidden personality which filters through Tadeo's diary as demoniac:

> Basta de tanta soberbia reprimida, de tanta sofrenada suficiencia, de tanta arrogancia oculta, pero, sobre todo, basta — porque no hay quien lo sufra ya — de esa mordacidad que, como un ácido, destruye cuanto toca. ¡Qué atroz — y qué imprevisto — resulta el Tadeo Requena de las memorias! ... Su verdadero talento, su fuerza, era de índole distinta, y muy temible por cierto: demoníaca. Consistía en el poder corrosivo de una mirada que volatiliza, disipa, vacía, corrompe, destruye, en fin, todos los objetos donde se posa, dejándolos reducidos a su pura apariencia irrisoria; poder tremendo, del que quizás él mismo no se daba cuenta, o no se daba cuenta cabal, como si, con una especie de rayos equis, viera la calavera bajo la carne, y una absurda danza de esqueletos en los movimientos de la gente; poder que ejercía sin proponérselo, sin quererlo, y que a saber si no se volvió contra sí propio y fue la causa profunda de su fracaso último, pues ¿dónde y cómo se detiene la cadena de la desintegración? [903-04]

Although Pinedo rejects Tadeo's narrative attitude, he does not consider it intentional or self-conscious, but rather uncanny and uncontrolled, whereas his own narrative attitude is calculated. Tadeo is cast here as a blind seer who, while penetrating the disguises of others remains blind to his own fate, which he so clearly foreshadows, and helpless to change its course. As he confesses in admitting to Doña Concha's ability to manipulate him at will: "La verdad es que no acierto a ver claro, ni consigo imaginarme cuál podrá ser la salida de este laberinto." [985] The roots of his destruction lie within himself, as do Pinedo's within him. In attributing to Tadeo the power to detect "la calavera bajo la carne, y una absurda danza de esqueletos en los movimientos de la gente," Pinedo strongly recalls his own language in referring to society's "grotesca danza de la muerte."

Tadeo's power of observation makes him the ideal chronicler since he sees both surface and interior in a single glance, although Pinedo is engaging in this same sort of internal penetration in his characterization of Tadeo. Both Tadeo and Pinedo make clear the detachment from the contemporary scene to which they owe their talent as observers. Pinedo, writing from the seclusion of his own room, attributes to his illness the spectator role which enables him to "see, perceive, and capture" what others fail to notice. [864] Tadeo, observing from the wings of the scene itself, comments on his presence at a ceremonial function:

> me gusta balconear esta clase de espectáculos, como le he hecho hoy, no desde el salón, ni siquiera desde la tribuna de invitados, sino desde la penumbra de algún rincón ignorado que me permita ver sin ser visto. [903]

The vantage point of both outsiders is the same; their role in society allows both to see without being seen, to echo Tadeo's words.

Of the two major narrators, Tadeo is the more sympathetic both by virtue of Pinedo's interest in him and because of his more intimate self-presentation which occasionally verges on introspection. His afternoon with Ángelo, his verbal defense of Luisito Rosales, even his inarticulateness following Rosales' funeral and his encounter with María Elena, as well as his inability to cope with the obviously malicious scheming of Doña Concha — all bring the reader into much closer contact with the inner Tadeo than he ever experiences with Pinedo, except perhaps in the closing chapter of the manuscript. Tadeo himself, in resuming his diary entries sometime after Rosales' death, views his writing as an act of self-confession: "ahora continúo casi por penitencia, como esos trabajos que se cumplen con la intención de salvar el alma." [985] While Pinedo consistently evokes Olóriz's hold over him and the old man's capacity for destroying others, he offers no such graphic proof as that which Tadeo's diary reveals about the equally capricious Doña Concha. In Pinedo's case, essentially his own fear compounded by his guilt feelings lead him to break down in front of Olóriz; out of the resultant feeling of humiliation grows the desire for revenge. While Tadeo initially is another Macbeth — Pinedo himself compares Doña Concha with a Shakespearean heroine [864] — Pinedo's downfall stems from his appropriation of Tadeo Requena's savings, an assertion of his sense of superiority over his fellow men and of his invulnerability to detection. Both men, when confronted with themselves, with the baseness of their motivating force and the weakness of their character, react violently to destroy the accuser, Tadeo responding instinctively and Pinedo, coldly. Tadeo in turn seems calmed in a sense of relief and finality, while Pinedo's emotions rise to an exalted, irrational pitch.

The reader, therefore, identifies more closely with Tadeo's emotional struggles: his inability to break away from Doña Concha's grip, his immediate and unyielding response to Bocanegra's challenge, his acceptance of approaching fate tempered by his need to communicate his perception of these final events. As Tadeo's benefactor and protector, Antón Bocanegra should perhaps elicit the reader's sympathy, for fundamentally Tadeo's action is the basest form of treachery as well as probable patricide, and Tadeo himself suggests that he instinctively murders Bocanegra in an attempt to eliminate the latter's accusatory stare. [1003] Given the atmosphere in which the events of the novel transpire and the lack of any positive perspective on Bocanegra — except relatively, in Pinedo's rectification of his earlier total condemnation — this is not so. Antón Bocanegra, alone, hated, feared and perhaps even misunderstood at the center of all the intrigue [6] remains only an empty

---

[6] Ayala, "El fondo sociológico en mis novelas," p. 546. Ayala has further suggested the comparison between Bocanegra and the figure of Carlos II as evoked in his best-known short story, "El hechizado," specifying it as:

una comparación que podría ilustrar bien mi manera de ver el poder sobre la tierra: tanto en el caso del rey legítimo como en el

figure for the reader, as his name suggests. Thus despite the murder, Tadeo has the reader at his side, the distance which Pinedo attempts to establish between them with his negative portrayal of Tadeo called into question by the increasingly evident parallelism between the two. Yet the cruelty of Tadeo's character, a defensive measure as he makes plain, cannot be downplayed, especially in his treatment of Luisito Rosales, the man to whom he owes his ability to persist in governmental circles. Strikingly, Pinedo employs the same metaphor in describing both Tadeo's situation and his own; while Tadeo writes "como si llevara una jauría a los talones," a pack of hounds which eventually overtakes him [985], Pinedo attempts to "disimularse entre la jauría, en evitación de que, un día u otro, a falta de más apetecibles piezas...." [1014] Both men are forced onto the defensive, and the animal imagery which underlies the entire narration, regardless of the narrator, suggests the less than human nature of this existence.

Pinedo arouses considerably less reader identification than Tadeo, despite the dominance of his first-person presentation, for the narrative offers no redeeming insights into his character. He is driven by fear, despite his superior tone and the superiority of his self-evaluation, and he has calculatedly attached himself to the man whose machinations cause him to ultimately destroy himself. Pinedo murders out of humiliation and frustration over his weakness when questioned by Olóriz not, like Tadeo's confrontation with Bocanegra, about murder, but about his probing into the events of the Bocanegra regime and the source of his new affluence. Ironically, Pinedo immediately assumes that the scheming Olóriz is making oblique references to the money Pinedo has appropriated from Tadeo via Sobrarbe, and instantly blames Sobrarbe for having denounced him, whereas it is also possible that Olóriz has only Loreto's reports of her conversations with Pinedo to go on when he confronts him. Thus while, like Tadeo, Pinedo responds out of guilt, his response takes the form of total capitulation to the insinuations of the accuser and his revenge, when it comes, plays in turn on the other man's fear, so similar to his own, belying the

---

del usurpador, el centro de todo el aparato del mando es una boca negra, un hueco sombrío, el vacío, el abismo.... en el fondo de la esfinge [Bocanegra] sospechamos, entrevemos el lote lamentable de la miseria que aflige a los hijos de Eva.

omnipotence which Pinedo has attributed to him. Pinedo had earlier delighted in capitalizing on Sobrarbe's fears, comparing himself with the rat catching the mouse, leading Sobrarbe to deliver both manuscript and money to him; Olóriz, in turn, produces in him the same hurried divestment of both items.

Weakness, then, is the tragic flaw which leads both Tadeo and Pinedo to their self-destruction, a weakness each only half acknowledges. Backed into corners by personalities more forceful than their own, both feel guilt for a crime already committed and, when faced with the accusation, choose to murder their accuser, thus freeing themselves from the most immediate source of danger. Despite Pinedo's negative perspective on Tadeo, in the end only the similarity of their vulnerability as human beings endures for the reader. Pinedo pinpoints the nature of Tadeo's fateful inability to respond to his approaching fate:

> Diríase que nuestro hombre fue víctima de una fatalidad ineluctible, capaz de moverlo en contra de las más firmes propensiones de su carácter, y aun en contra de su instinto, que lo hacía reacio. [928]

In retrospect at least, Pinedo clearly detects the inexorable movement of the hand of fate. As he observes in describing Doña Concha's death, "hay casos en que hubiera sido menester casi un milagro para torcer destino tan perfectamente previsible, dadas las circunstancias." [863] In attributing the major coincidences and the weaknesses of human nature to fate, Pinedo diffuses any possible reader disbelief, avoiding as well the pitfalls of melodrama, by offering the reader an explanation for circumstances which might otherwise be difficult to accept. At the same time, Pinedo's frequent interjections on the strange nature of events — " ¡Buena caja de sorpresas es el mundo; y bien de ellas encierran las tales memorias! " [864] — prepare the reader to have his credulity tested. The degree to which control lies outside the individual results from the portrayal of each human life as flawed and manipulated by others, while the insistence on the force of fate relieves the individual of responsibility for his actions and denies the reader the right to declare him guilty.

Since Pinedo's tone and self-portrayal have not drawn the reader's sympathy in the first twenty-nine chapters — indeed the detached, ironic tone has drawn him increasingly away from the narrator — the abjectness of his responses in the final chapter do nothing to reverse this stand. Even after murdering Olóriz, Pinedo's humiliation lingers on: "Aún no me explico — la verdad — por qué se me confió así. ¿En tan poco me tenía?" [1017] The realization comes as a shock to Pinedo's self-esteem; Tadeo answers essentially the same question with a bullet. Pinedo's final line as it babbles on about his heroic nature, which the reader views in juxtaposition to his base behavior, seals the volume on a peak of irony. And Pinedo's dictum, proffered in the context of defending himself against the accusation of having participated in Camarasa's death, sounds again in the reader's ears:

> Cada cual es el autor de su propia suerte; cada uno es el primer y principal responsable de lo que venga a sucederle. No se puede ser impunemente tan desatentado como él era. [877]

The structure if not the themes of the novel seems to uphold Pinedo's harsh view, and there is no doubt as to Pinedo's own future in the heavily weighted atmosphere of retribution, both human and extra-human (the theme of fate runs throughout the novel). Further, the punishment frequently seems designed to fit the crime, as is especially clear in the deaths of Olóriz and Doña Concha and in Pancho Cortina's incapacitation. But the reader does not condemn Pinedo for his weakness or false pride, for the inability to see himself clearly; the reader is simply too distant from Pinedo either to applaud or feel repulsed by his actions. The reader's role is to accept them as further examples of the reduction of human life to its most elemental emotions in the dehumanizing atmosphere of the novel.

A self-conscious narrator, Pinedo consciously manipulates the structure of his presentation and, concomitantly, the reader's response. On a deeper level, it is the implied author standing behind Pinedo who points to the parallels, engages in foreshadowing and plays the ironist from a perspective above the narrator's own viewpoint. Pinedo's textual commentary on the documents and on his developing text guides the reader in his task as he applies himself to the novel as a whole. Thus as a narrator Pinedo elucidates the reader's path toward the position of the implied author. While the reader must participate not only in accepting the verisimilitude of the narration but in building his relationship to the text, he is provided with ample, clearly marked guideposts in this journey. The implied author invites the reader's company as always, but additionally in *Muertes de perro* he takes few chances of missing it. Despite the ironies, there is little chance that the reader will not follow the role marked out for him and stand by the implied author's side.

Chapter III

EL FONDO DEL VASO: THE UNCONSCIOUS NARRATOR

The narrative structure of *El fondo del vaso* is segmented, separating into three distinct parts, with the narrative plane unfolding chronologically to span all three: 1) José Lino Ruiz's first-person manuscript, largely in the form of a diary;[1] 2) a series of newspaper clippings from a local paper *El Comercio* covering the death of Luis Rodríguez Junior with which José Lino Ruiz is initially charged; 3) José Lino's inner monologue or dialogue with himself from his prison cell. Although the narrative technique and focus of each part is unique, José Lino emerges as the pivotal figure whose slow and painful process of self-awareness unites his written and oral narratives, while the intervening journalistic interlude evokes a broader spectrum of society. The shifting narrative perspectives elicit their corresponding reader response, as the distance between narrator and reader varies. Although strictly speaking only José Lino's narratives come under the purview of this study, the newspaper articles present certain similarities to first-person narration, as will be shown.

Undertaken to rectify Luis Pinedo's negative projection of President Antón Bocanegra in his published treatise, *Muertes de perro,* José Lino Ruiz's manuscript comprising Part I of *El fondo del vaso* follows the development of this project to the writing stage before the focus shifts to a series of incidents from José Lino's own life initially arising out of his literary project. An emotional crisis in

---

[1] The definition of the diary form discussed in relation to *Muertes de perro* applies to Part I of *El fondo del vaso* as well; see Chapter II, note 3.

his deteriorating relationship with his mistress, Candelaria Gómez, the consistently mystifying actions of his wife Corina, the rise and fall of his friendship with his literary mentor, Luis R. Rodríguez, or a social situation whose full significance disturbingly seems to elude him, motivate José Lino to record his responses in an attempt to comprehend and control the factors which, despite his efforts, are working to change his life situation. Certain settings of these crisis points — the festival of "la Federación de Artistas de Cine, Televisión, etc.," the "miss INCOLO" competition to represent the "asociación de la Industria y el Comercio Locales," and Don Cipriano Medrano's liquor emporium — contribute to the underlying social satire broadened in Part II to incorporate other classes and institutions of society. The newspaper clippings link José Lino to the murder of his former mistress's boy-friend Junior Rodríguez, recording his vain attempts to escape implication followed by his arrest. Ultimately, the police stumble upon what again appear to be the actual circumstances of Junior's death through the incorporation of a new perspective which in turn frees José Lino from suspicion, but not before his personal and public life lie in shambles. From the depths of financial and moral ruination, compounded by the emotional desolation of Corina's totally unexpected (to him) confession of infidelity, José Lino ultimately achieves total self-awareness in the monologue comprising the last part of the novel. After an examination of the link between the two novels, this chapter treats the role of the narrator and the reader response in Part I of *El fondo del vaso* before moving to a consideration of the remaining two parts of the novel.

A. Part I

Linked to *Muertes de perro* by the reappearance of three characters mentioned only briefly by Luis Pinedo, who either declares them dead or in economic ruin, *El fondo del vaso* unfolds in the same fictitious Central American banana republic at some years' distance from the terminal event of the earlier novel, Pinedo's murder of Olóriz. An "Asesinado Superviviente" [1024] now returned from his "viaje a Ultratumba," José Lino Ruiz serves as the narrative consciousness through which the novel initially and ultimately filters. Believed to have been a victim of the chaotic aftermath of President Antón Bocanegra's murder, José Lino is disparagingly characterized in passing by Pinedo as, "el bobo de José Lino, con quien no se podía hablar dos palabras seguidas sobre cosa alguna" [876]. Pinedo depicts him as an innocent, if hardly likeable, victim whose only crime has been a social one, his "inocentes carambolas" [863] in La Aurora:

> ¿cómo no suponer, por ejemplo, que al majadero de José Lino Ruiz (Dios lo haya perdonado) lo que le costó el pellejo fueron — pues ¡qué otra cosa iba a ser! — sus ufanas series de interminables carambolas en el Gran Café y Billares de La Aurora...? [862]

Assigned an obscure and absurd role in Pinedo's cynical view of society, the entrepreneur José Lino Ruiz, sole owner of Casa Ruiz, Grandes Almacenes de Ramos Generales, as narrator of his own life indirectly substantiates Pinedo's description of him. Further, José Lino's own name contributes to the diminution of his importance as an individual in the reader's eyes, since phonetically the second name serves as a diminutive suffix converting José into "Joselino." In the earlier novel, Pinedo records that others refer to him as "Pinedito"; here the reader must perceive the effect of the double name in detracting from José Lino's stature.

Two other important citizens whose disappearance from society Pinedo recorded in *Muertes de perro* resurface in *El fondo del vaso* in secondary roles: the financier, Doménech, ruined by Bocanegra, and the newspaperman Luis R. Rodríguez, "murdered" according to Pinedo for his "gramatiquerías puntillosas en las columnas de *El Comercio*" [862]. Author of "palmetazos pedantes" [863], Rodríguez sports the less than illustrious double appelative Rodríguez Rodríguez. "El gallego Rodríguez," as both narrators refer to him, also figures in *Muertes de perro* as the author of "una letrilla, bastante mala por cierto, llena de los cien mil disparates, pero no menos colmada de ironías punzantes" [882], written on the occasion of Luis Rosales' acceptance of the portfolio of Minister of Education. In line with Pinedo's negative appraisal of Rodríguez's versification, Tadeo Requena cites him as the fastidious ghost writer of the native poet laureate's verses, questioning sarcastically in his diary:

> por mucho que los maldicientes se rieran de que en la redacción el gallego Rodríguez le tenía que corregir [a Camilo Zapato] la ortografía y algún que otro verso mal contado, ¿por qué no los escribía [los versos] el gallego, si tan capaz era? [902]

Rodríguez's participation in Camilo Zapato's literary career prefigures his role as José Lino's literary mentor in the opening chapter of *El fondo del vaso* and his displays of dubious erudition on matters of vocabulary. José Lino's consistently exaggerated praise of Rodríguez's literary talent in the early pages of his narrative derives its ironic humor for the reader from comparison with Rodríguez's pedantic, verbose discourses on writing, recorded by José Lino, and additionally, for the reader familiar with the preceding narrative, with Pinedo's and Tadeo Requena's appraisals of his capabilities.

In attesting to the continuing existence of José Lino Ruiz and Luis R. Rodríguez and to the circumstances of Doménech's life following his financial ruin, *El fondo del vaso* corrects the "truth" as presented in Pinedo's manuscript by the addition of José Lino's perspective. In addition José Lino enlarges on the perspectives incorporated into *Muertes de perro* by his rejection of Pinedo's portrayal of the Bocanegra era. The emergence of José Lino as narrator yields the unique and dissenting perspective of a "victim" of the post-Bocanegra triumvirate who left the country rather than suffer possible economic loss. With the concurrence and support of his fellow returnee from beyond the pale, he decides to write a *reivindicación* [2] of Bocanegra in answer to *Muertes de perro*. To the irony of a former corpse undertaking to vindicate Bocanegra's image is counterbalanced the irony of José Lino's confession that "el proverbial viaje que — por allanarme a la broma — he llamado a Ultratumba... en verdad no alcanzó a pasar de la capital azteca" [1051]. As for his literary mentor Rodríguez, José Lino contemptuously records that the Galician quite ignominiously "se había pasado un mes largo agazapado en el sótano de la tienda de un paisano suyo" [1024]. Both of these early revelations detract from

---

[2] José Lino Ruiz employs the term *reivindicación* which this study will translate as "vindication," although the translation is broader than the legal focus of the original.

the heroic potential of the two principal characters of *El fondo del vaso,* adding to their ridiculousness in the eyes of a reader already primed by Pinedo — either directly or through quotations included in José Lino's manuscript — to accept this view. Thus even if the reader is not familiar with Pinedo's earlier narrative, its viewpoint is present in the later volume as José Lino and Rodríguez record in outrage Pinedo's mocking accusations of their crimes to demonstrate the gross injustice of his perspective and substantiate the need to vindicate Bocanegra, and incidentally themselves, from the warped presentation of *Muertes de perro.*

José Lino's motivation to vindicate Bocanegra's name initially arises in response to Pinedo's narrative, which he characterizes, paraphrasing Rodríguez, as "pieza de la más refinada perfidia" [1027]. In commenting on the publication of this work which, he reports, occurred after Pinedo's trial for the murder of Olóriz — a fact which the reader of *Muertes de perro* had to assume in accepting his access to the text José Lino establishes its autonomy, granting it an existence apart from either his or Pinedo's narrative. Standing outside the novelistic world of *Muertes de perro,* José Lino comments on it, viewing it as a publication, as does the reader, although not as fiction but as a historical document. Enhancing the autonomy of the work is the inclusion in José Lino's narrative of quotations from actual reviews of *Muertes de perro.* In reviewing to himself Pinedo's distortion of the Bocanegra era, José Lino incorporates a series of descriptive phrases which "críticos diversos" [1031] have employed in describing the atmosphere of the Bocanegra regime as portrayed by Pinedo. As Rosario Hiriart has shown, these quotations derive from two early reviews of *Muertes de perro*[3] in newspapers of Puerto Rico where Ayala was then residing. José Lino utilizes the phraseology of these reviews

---

[3] *Las alusiones literarias en la obra narrativa de Francisco Ayala* (New York: Las Américas, 1972), pp. 93-96. Hiriart raises the question of whether or not Ayala accepts the quoted criticism of his novel by citing from Part II of the *Quijote* a discussion of Part I, concluding:

> Parece que acepta Cervantes la crítica a su novela intercalada ["El curioso impertinente"] y, no obstante, si leemos *bien,* veremos que no la acepta nada. Con esto creo haber contestado a la pregunta.

p. 96. An understanding of José Lino's relationship to these quotations is the necessary first step in determining the position of the implied author.

to uphold his contention about the reader's response to Pinedo's narrative, maintaining: "carece de toda base real esa impresión truculenta que, sin embargo, logra [Pinedo] transmitir" [1031]. Through these quotations not only José Lino but the implied author are clearly commenting on the negative response to the Bocanegra era, a response which to the implied author is as much without foundation as is José Lino's positive presentation. Ironically, José Lino uses the actual phraseology of the reviewers to support his pro-Bocanegra viewpoint, thus clearly showing the distance between the two evaluations. His declaration that "es mínimo el catálogo de atrocidades que recoge Pinedo, por muy aglomeradas que las presente," demonstrates his bias, while the critic who writes of the "clima inmoral" under the regime expresses the opposite bias [1031].

At a later point in his narration José Lino cites by author a review of *Muertes de perro* from a Buenos Aires newspaper, extracting from it the metaphorical assessment of the narrative act based on the proverb "por la boca muere el pez" [1048].[4] Even as Pinedo and Tadeo Requena reveal their true selves in their narratives, both through unconscious indirection and, on a more literal level, through their written confessions of murder, José Lino runs the same risk in his narrative. Despite this awareness, but unaware that he has already revealed himself for what he is, José Lino feels the compulsion to continue his entries:

> sigo dándole a la pluma para hablar de cien mil tonterías, de todo y de nada, de cuanto se me viene a las mientes, aun a sabiendas de que ello es inútil y vano, y quizá sólo para mi propio perjuicio (no sea que se diga también de mí lo que un escritor argentino, Nalé Roxlo, ha sentenciado acerca de Pinedito y del mismo Requena: que *por la boca muere el pez*). [1047-48]

---

[4] Contrary to the impression that the inclusion of this proverb in José Lino's narrative may leave, it does not constitute a direct quotation from the review of *Muertes de perro,* which simply alludes to the proverb in characterizing Pinedo and Tadeo Requena:

> Estos peces chapoteantes en el fango ambiente, como los del refrán, mueren también por la boca, descubriendo en las entrelíneas lo que en las líneas, a veces, pretendían ocultar.

Hiriart, *Las alusiones literarias,* p. 95.

Implicit in José Lino's confession is the acknowledgement of potential reader access to his manuscript, paralleling the fate of the earlier manuscripts. Although neither within the context of *El fondo del vaso* nor implicitly outside its immediate context does José Lino's narrative reach a reader's hands, this acknowledgement of potential reader response is significant in revealing José Lino's awareness of the need for the narrative control in which he is completely lacking.

José Lino's references to the published volume *Muertes de perro* do not fully coincide with the reader's image of it, since the reader realizes that each individual attains only a partial view of reality and thus considers the work a collection of divergent, personal perspectives. As for the importance of the contents, José Lino asserts that at the time of its publication,

> todos los documentos que integran el volumen, o los principales, habían visto ya antes la luz en los diarios, al menos en extracto, con ocasión del proceso Pinedo. [1027]

José Lino's qualifying phrases concerning the published form of the documents are basic to the difference between his response to *Muertes de perro* and the reader's. This admission of the editing of the documents reveals that the press has engaged in the same manipulations as Pinedo, since any selection derives from an implicit interpretation and results in distortion. Thus in neither case has the public had access to the full documentation. As Rodríguez distinguishes in his lengthy dissertation paraphrased by José Lino, perspective and not the documents themselves holds the key to *Muertes de perro,* since no fault can be raised with the publication of documents in themselves. The absence of editorial comment has lead readers to view *Muertes de perro* as documented truth, since:

> Hipócritamente, sus editores lo habían publicado sin otro comentario que ese título torpe e impropio, pero sugestivo, con el carácter, inocuo en apariencia, de la pura documentación. [1027]

The title, of course, arises from the text itself, as there are numerous episodes with canine participants, and from the basic imagery, so that it is in effect an extension of Pinedo's perspective, as well as the perspective of the implied author. The emphasis on the absence of any further editorial presence relates to the reader's response to the novels *Muertes de perro* and *El fondo del vaso,* to be discussed later.

Rodríguez argues that in writing a rebuttal of Pinedo's work, José Lino must follow Pinedo's lead and turn the narrative perspective to his own advantage. By assailing Pinedo's interpretation, rather than the documents themselves, he can negate the documentary nature of *Muertes de perro* and thus:

> Poner de relieve que los editores del dichoso volumen, lejos de haberse limitado a ofrecer inocentemente al público, según pretenden, una colección de documentos oficiales, o hechos tales por el sacramento judicial, de los que ni siquiera una línea han tachado, el objetivo que persiguen es el muy perverso de dar pábulo a la común malignidad que siempre hace leña del árbol caído [Antón Bocanegra]. [1028]

Beyond this José Lino must attack the documents at their only weak point — Pinedo's manipulation of them:

> lo malo es la selección de los hechos que el atravesado de su autor tuvo a bien recoger, la relación en que los presenta, la luz a que los pone, lo que deja entender y lo que omite. [1029]

In contrast to José Lino's initially sincere, if naive, desire to vindicate Bocanegra, Rodríguez stands at a sufficient distance from the project, both by virtue of his greater experience as a writer and his ulterior motive in agreeing to aid José Lino, to assess clearly the required approach. Not historical "truth" but limited, individual perspective is involved, and the manipulation of perspective requires a degree of detachment from the subject, such as Pinedo evidenced up to the last pages of his manuscript.

Luis Rodríguez's long-winded observations on *Muertes de perro,* which José Lino records in his first entry, function to reveal Rodríguez's character and, by virtue of the contrast between his distanced views and José Lino's ingenuous support of Bocanegra, furnish the reader a perspective on José Lino's character at the same time. Additionally, Rodríguez's commentary on the relationship between "truth" and narrative perspective incorporates a response to the narrative technique and tone of the earlier work which helps to illuminate the present text as well. Rodríguez's participation in the narration as José Lino's close friend and mentor allows the reader to respond directly to him and to comprehend precisely what escapes the narrator: the reason for Rodríguez's frequent presence in his home. The projected vindication of Bocanegra justifies the existence of José Lino's manuscript by establishing the context in which his interest in writing develops and by tracing his attempts at written self-expression. Thus it sets the stage for his credibility as narrator as well as for his limited, unselfconscious narrative perspective.

From abject praise of Rodríguez's abilities, and from the belief that he, José Lino, first envisioned the literary project, promoting it in turn to his wife and to Rodríguez, José Lino comes later to recognize that:

> En el fondo, creo que nunca me interesó demasiado, y que si me metí en la empresa fue por sugestión de Corina y, sobre todo, por la oficiosa insistencia de ese mismo Rodríguez que ahora se ha echado atrás. [1047]

In absolving himself of responsibility for the failure to complete the project, José Lino reverses his earlier enthusiastic position, ironically hitting upon the combination of factors which his wife Corina and Rodríguez have manipulated in their favor to facilitate their relationship. But José Lino is writing out of pique, transferring the blame to other shoulders, without any realization of the truth his words contain.

The written narrative constituting Part I of *El fondo del vaso* falls into five chapter divisions, each comprised of a series of undated entries and each bearing a title which reflects the central concern of the entries. The distance and detachment from the narrative which these summary headings imply indicate to the reader that they have been added by an editorial hand. Following the pattern of José Lino's emotional responses, the entries cluster at emotional peaks. As he confesses near the end of his manuscript concerning the sporadic nature of his entries:

> A veces, escribo horas seguidas en [estos cuadernos]; y a veces se me pasan días, cuando no meses, sin agregar una línea; hasta que de pronto me vuelve la urgencia de des-

> ahogarme, y entonces leo el último párrafo, si acaso, o un par de ellos, para ponerme a tono y, enlazando ahí de cualquier manera, continúo tan campante, sin preocuparme demasiado de que venga a cuento o no lo que escribo con todo lo anterior. [1098]

As José Lino records, the link between entries is tangential, but his concern over coherence and structural unity, albeit theoretical, reveals an implicit reader orientation not associated with the diary format but consistent with the originally planned text vindicating Bocanegra. In any event, the observations on the timespan of the narrative plane and on structure seem to serve the reader by justifying the narrative structure. Once José Lino turns entirely inward in his entries, they flow more consistently around a central conflict: his relationship with Candelaria Gómez. As in Pinedo's narrative, the overall chronology is vague, while the temporal relationship between events remains precise. Instead of allowing each episode to develop on a daily basis, the cluster effect places José Lino in a position of retrospection, recording the development and complication of an episode from the crisis point. The dual temporal perspective of retrospection and immediacy is maintained throughout, as José Lino views the events leading up to the narrative present in the light of his present circumstances. Thus both his immediate action and his delayed reaction, both his expectation and the result, are recorded. While generally close to the events of the action plane, with the exception of the opening section in which the narrative lag extends to several years, the narrative retains the distance implicit in a written review of the day's events from the perspective of evening.

Although José Lino's manuscript, like Pinedo's, is originally conceived as a rough draft of a volume planned to elicit a specific reader response, this projected reader orientation dissipates once José Lino acknowledges that he is producing an intimate personal record or self-confession rather than a public vindication of Bocanegra. Indeed, José Lino's narrative takes on the characteristics of a dialogue between the two halves of José Lino's personality: one spontaneous, emotional and weak; the other distanced, pragmatic and strong. Even before he formally abandons his original intent, most of what he has recorded bears on himself rather than on Bocanegra. Only the paragraph which Rodríguez contributes and

José Lino's recurring paens to his mentor are clearly reader-oriented, although José Lino's early self-revelations are in essence frustrated public confessions which he cannot voice aloud.

Despite Rodríguez's expansiveness he offers José Lino little concrete help, as José Lino increasingly notes. However, it is only after reading some ten pages that the reader is informed of Rodríguez's one written contribution to their literary endeavor: the opening paragraph of the manuscript, which he has cast in José Lino's voice. José Lino comes to this declaration only after detailing in the opening section of the manuscript the genesis and development of the project of *reivindicación* to the point at which Rodríguez, ignoring José Lino's own prepared introduction, presents him with an opening paragraph. The self-deprecatory "a fuer de tonto que soy" [1021] contained in this paragraph takes on a new dimension when viewed as coming from Rodríguez, albeit writing as José Lino, and not as a self-characterization. In ironic juxtaposition Rodríguez evokes the "avieso, inteligentísimo Pinedo," underscoring the reversal of roles in his execution and the narrative act in the hands of José Lino and Rodríguez, the "difuntos apócrifos" [1022]. The initial reference to Rodríguez takes on an ironic dimension as well, coming as it does from his own pen as a defense of his own reputation. Describing Pinedo's narrative style to José Lino, Rodríguez contemptuously asserts that, after opening his narration with "frases retóricas de alcance general, y por lo mismo imprecisas, engañadoras," and with "remontadas prosopopeyas," Pinedo soon had to abandon these and lapse into "repugnantes vulgaridades de estilo" [1029]. The remark applies as well to the rhetoric of Rodríguez's opening paragraph, directed to Pinedo as a challenge to the truth of his narrative. The remarks also serve as an ironic commentary by the implied author on the style of the earlier novel.

Despite the narrative distance from events of from several years to several months from which José Lino writes his initial entries, he nevertheless records conversations in either direct or indirect form, including Rodríguez's lengthy monologues on the subject of Pinedo's book. To substantiate his recollection of Rodríguez's ideas, he refers to informal notes taken at the time [1028], while Rodríguez talked. Only when unable to comprehend the sudden cooling of Rodríguez's friendship, incomprehensible to him since he has never fathomed that the basis of the friendship lay in Rodríguez's relationship with his wife, José Lino attempts to explain it as a blank in his memory, the result of having imbibed too much [1029]; in effect, if he cannot comprehend a situation, then the cause must lie outside his control. In drawing attention to the problem of recall, José Lino builds credibility for the detailed nature of his entries. This credibility is especially crucial to his recording of his dream. Here again he posits that his inability to recall the total dream may be the cause of its fragmented nature and incoherence [1090]. Aside from these special circumstances in which lapses in memory are comprehensible, José Lino evidences an excellent memory, making him an invaluable, reliable narrator capable of communicating more than he fully comprehends. Commenting in Part III, José Lino contrasts his lack of comprehension of certain events with their continuing presence on his mind:

> la cuestión es esta: si todavía me acuerdo con tanta precisión de ese diálogo mudo, ¿cómo es que entonces lo pasé por alto? Lo pasé por alto, igual que lee uno a veces sin enterarse párrafos enteros de un libro, porque al mismo tiempo está pensando en otra cosa. [1173]

In answering his own question, José Lino is providing credibility for the basic narrative technique underlying his narration, by confirming the plausibility of his being able to recall events without ever seeing their significance. Indeed, his blindness to the true content of his writing renders him a faithful transcriber, since he cannot be thought to have altered anything in an effort to change its impact. But it is essential that he record words and actions despite their seeming senselessness to him, and here his awareness of intellectual inferiority comes into play. Realizing that others think of him as "tonto," "necio" or "bobo," José Lino struggles to grasp the significance of what is happening around him, relating in his diary those comments and events which puzzle him. This facet of his personality, the desire to know what others know, upholds his eventual confrontation with himself in Part III. José Lino's inflated self-confidence in matters of business and love is readily identified by the reader as a distorted self-image and is easily separated from the essence of what he records. By clearly revealing his personal assessment, José Lino allows the reader to detect both his perspective and the perspective of others.

In one respect José Lino is a self-conscious narrator: with respect to his literary ability. Despite his initial admiration for his friend Rodríguez's talent, he early remarks on his own response to the unaccustomed task: "Escribir no es tan difícil, después de todo: basta con ponerse a ello" [1027]. Flattered initially by Rodríguez into believing he can write a book, José Lino becomes increasingly defensive of his own abilities as the flattery diminishes along with Rodríguez's interest. To account for the increased mastery with which he expresses himself and in recognition of his debt to his mentor, whose words he finds himself echoing in a constant reminder of Rodríguez's imprint on his life — although he only partially perceives that imprint — José Lino declares: "la verdad es que si uno se dedica a escribir, sea o no en secreto, es natural que poco a poco se le vaya refinando el lenguaje" [1068]. Both Rodríguez's earlier presence in his life and the Galician's observations on writing allow José Lino to develop an ability for self-expression which does not clash with his prior image as thickheaded. José Lino's need for an outlet for his thoughts and an opportunity for reflection lead him to continue the diary even after abandoning the vindication of Bocanegra, without causing any surprise to the reader.

The recurrence of the image *renacuajo* in conjunction with Pinedo clearly illustrates the distance between Rodríguez and José Lino, as well as the mentor's influence on the pupil, and between the narrators of *Muertes de perro* and *El fondo del vaso*. Pinedo introduces into his narrative Tadeo's reference to him as "ese renacuajo de Pinedito" [916] without any further comment than in turn to cite Tadeo as "el cachafaz." In addition to the figurative meaning of a small, despicable person, *renacuajo* on a metaphorical level presents a cruelly appropriate image of Pinedo's physique. In refuting Pinedo's unflattering obituaries of José Lino and himself, Rodríguez picks up on this graphic epithet, which appears only once in the earlier volume, in his opening paragraph, providing in addition the following definition:

> (Renacuajo significa — y para quien lo ignore, así lo aclara la Academia — la cría de la rana, que no teniendo aún

patas, se mueve, sin embargo, en el agua cual ágil pez.) [1022]

Only Rodríguez, his reader in mind, feels the need to provide a definition, citing the Academy dictionary as his source like someone who has just looked up the word himself. His definition spells out the image, highlighting the aspects fundamental to Tadeo's visualization of the comparison between the crippled Pinedo and a tadpole: the manner and efficacy of movement. Immediately following, Rodríguez strings out a series of similar epithets in an apostrofe to Pinedo by antonomasia: "sí, señor Renacuajo, o Gusarapo, o Escuerzo...." Although similar on one level, the two additional nicknames do not fulfill the same function as Tadeo's original use of *renacuajo*. By associating the three, Rodríguez reduces them to their common denominator of water-dwelling and hence repulsive creatures, drawing increasingly away from the sharpness of the original image. By vaunting his erudition and, concomitantly assuming the reader's lack of it, Rodríguez has merely demonstrated more blatantly that he has missed the point.

The additional names supplied by Rodríguez continue to appear in *El fondo del vaso*. Rodríguez himself creates an original image from them in reference to the project of discrediting *Muertes de perro* by transferring the image from Pinedo to his manuscript: "ese engendro o renacuajo de libro se escurre entre las manos, y casi no hay manera de cogerlo en renuncio" [1028]. In this case the two images are equally graphic, while demonstrating clearly the change Rodríguez has introduced in adopting the metaphor *renacuajo* from Tadeo. José Lino carries this process one step further, destroying completely the parallelism between the three epithets as well as the original image, by substituting a synonym in his reference to Pinedo as "el pobre sapo" [1033]. The linguistic simplification from *escuerzo* to *sapo* is as characteristic of José Lino as the pedantry is of Luis Rodríguez.

Towards the end of Part I, José Lino makes reference to the possibility of his diary being read, referring to it as "un mamotreto monstruoso, informe" [1098]. In effect, he is attempting to view his narrative through an observer's eyes, and yet the reader's response to it is the opposite, finding it highly organized. But José Lino's assertion serves to introduce the suggestion of its shapelessness, more in keeping with the nature of a diary. The circumstances in which it might be read are not specified, but the mention of the possibility evokes the parallel with Pinedo's and Tadeo Requena's manuscripts, adding an ominous note as did the earlier reference to the proverbial death of a fish. Only in Part III does José Lino mirror the reader's perspective, as he attains the distance to view his earlier words and actions with the knowledge which the reader has possessed since he first grasped the nature of Rodríguez's friendship.

As José Lino turns back to review his life in a new light in Part III, so twice in Part I the reader is forced to return to the beginning and view what he has already read from a new perspective. First, upon learning that Rodríguez is the author of the opening paragraph of the manuscript, challenged by José Lino's affirmation that:

> probablemente el lector avezado haya descubierto en su prosa, no bien la recorriera con la vista, el estilo suntuoso, recargado y digno, en virtud del cual es tenida la firma de Luis R. Rodríguez por una de las más señeras en nuestro Parnaso. [1033]

And again when Corina reveals to José Lino, at his instigation, that she has known all along about his affair with Candelaria Gómez, confronting both José Lino and the reader with a different image of herself from the one he has projected to date in phrases of assumed superiority like "la pobre gata" [1023] and, referring specifically to her ignorance of his secretary's presence in Mexico, "este inocente ángel mío" [1024]. Suddenly José Lino's self-satisfied superiority towards his wife is shattered, while the reader has gradually come to realize the significance of her moodiness, which baffles José Lino, and to detect the correspondence between her moods and Rodríguez's moods. Thus in the first case José Lino has withheld information from the reader by not revealing the authorship of the opening lines until reaching the point at which they were written in his chronological recounting of the narrative's genesis; in the second case, José Lino, as well as the reader, is forced to shift his perspective, which nevertheless remains much more limited than the reader's.

In the opening section of José Lino's manuscript, the narrative distance shortens consistently as his account of the projected vindication draws closer to the narrative present from which he writes. Following a lapse of "days or months" he resumes his narrative, this time to reflect upon his self-appointed role as "cronista de ocasión, retórico improvisado, oficioso redentor," citing the lack of motivation to complete the task and, more revealingly, the absence of "el sentido de lo que conviene decir y de lo que es necesario callar" [1038] as deterrents to further progress. Both traits have almost from the first been highly apparent to the reader, but it is symptomatic of José Lino's lagging self-awareness that he only acknowledges these self-evident characteristics in his second entry. To date the manuscript has dealt with the process of writing a rebuttal to Pinedo's book without in any way constituting such a rebuttal, apart from Rodríguez's contribution. Even José Lino comes to admit this in his third entry after rereading his earlier writing: "Según compruebo al repasarlo, casi nada tiene que ver con la defensa del calumniado prócer" [1045], Rodríguez's estrangement, the cause of which escapes José Lino's comprehension, dooms the literary project. Concomitantly with the recognition of this fact, José Lino acknowledges that he is instead engaging in a personal record of his life, indicating his dependency upon this emotional outlet: "he aquí que sigo escribiendo; que continúo y continúo emborronando papeles. Se ve que he adquirido el vicio" [1047]. The reader is convinced of José Lino's need and ability to keep a diary, since in effect this is what he has been doing to date under a different pretext; thus the existence of the record itself becomes credible. His consistent inward focus finds expression.

In effect, a process which had already begun when Pinedo wrote his narrative is now completed. The temporal distance from the Bocanegra era has completely altered the late President's image in the public mind. Pinedo acknowledged that later atrocities had lent Bocanegra a retrospective stature. In José Lino's case, the intervening years of plenty — "los años de vacas gordas con que el cielo nos compensa de los sufrimientos, escaseces y violencias pretéritos" [1057] — have gradually erased the memory of the duress of the post-Bocanegra era:

> ...Bastante próximo aún en el tiempo según calendarios y relojes, todo ello se le presenta a la memoria un

tanto desteñido, destituido y lejano, porque — tan fecunda es la paz, tan próvidas sus cosechas — estos pocos años han modificado la faz de nuestro país hasta un punto tal que parecen remotas ya y casi inverosímiles sus estrecheces, penalidades y miserias de otrora. [1056]

Time has achieved what José Lino cannot: the emergence of a different perspective on Bocanegra. With this meditation on the passage of time, the figure of Bocanegra and the events of the following regime remain definitely in the past, and the narrative shifts permanently into the present concerns of José Lino's life, concerns which nevertheless arise directly out of his earlier actions. José Lino terminates his tribute to the good years at hand by stating that "nadie tiene derecho a desesperarse" [1056]. And yet that is precisely what happens to him by Part III of *El fondo del vaso*, the last link in an unbroken chain extending from the Bocanegra era into the narrative present of Part III.

In the second chapter of his manuscript, José Lino offers a detailed retrospective of his relationship with an employee, Candelaria (Candy) Gómez, in response to an event in the narrative present. Since the opening line of his part in the narrative José Lino has had Candy on his mind; his remarks on the ingratitude of "ciertos personajes o personajillos de nuestro ambiente" [1022] constitute a veiled reference to his largess on her behalf. In his first version of his "viaje a Ultratumba," he projects his cleverness in choosing the moment of greatest political instability for a long-desired vacation. When acquaintances raze him for this escape, he bridles, but cannot "let the cat out of the bag," as he confides in his diary, in a second version of this trip:

> Lo que más rabia me da con esta bobada es que, sin duda, no me considerarían tan tonto si supieran que en mi desaparición hubo gato encerrado. Claro que, de saberlo, ¿hasta dónde no llegaría su envidia? Pues es evidente que en todo esto lo que hay es algo y aun mucho de envidia; la cosa no tiene otra explicación. [1042]

Ironically, José Lino's well-guarded secret is common knowledge, and what he mistakes for envy are pointed references to the real nature of his escapade. Thus José Lino is not hero of this episode in his life, as he believes, but the brunt of a common joke; this is the "other explanation" which eludes him in his self-confidence. He feels himself superior to their comprehension of the facts and writes what he cannot express out loud: "desde luego, señores, no fue pura tontuna como ustedes — infelices — suponen, mi falso mutis de esta vida: sépanlo" [1042].

As José Lino's confidence in his ability to carry out the rebuttal to Pinedo's narrative and his friendship with Rodríguez wane, so does his self-assurance. The entire narrative, with its sequel in Part III, documents the disintegration of José Lino's self-image and his growing awareness of the distance between this image and the self he projects to others. A slap in the face from Candy in the narrative present jolts this self-confrontation along, as on the evening of this painful event he pours out in a defensive tone the history of their relationship in its third version. No longer the smug hero but the unappreciated, magnanimous benefactor, José Lino records a losing battle to regain Candy's dependence on him. The struggle itself is pointless, even from José Lino's perspective; he fully recognizes the root of his problem. He confesses to himself: "No tengo empacho en reconocer que, entre otras aprensiones, me acompañaba en mi regreso de Ultratumba la de... la debilidad mía con aquella Candelaria" [1056]. She poses two constant threats to his peace of mind: an increasing economic drain and possible blackmail. With Candy now pursued by a young man, precisely Luis Rodríguez's son, Junior Rodríguez, José Lino initially remains certain of the superiority and strength of his position. In an imaginary confrontation with the lovers, he addresses them condescendingly as "amiguitos míos" and threatens:

> Esta aborrecida metrópoli que se llama José Lino Ruiz cuenta con recursos más que suficientes para frustrar cualesquiera veleidades libertadoras de su colonia querida, y si alguna vez accede por fin a emanciparla, pueden estar seguros de que será mediante un acto magnánimo de su voluntad soberana y no por la fuerza de una rebeldía triunfadora ni mucho menos por ajena imposición. [1057]

Obviously José Lino is not bound to Candy by ties of love, but by a commercial spirit of possession; his pride and self-esteem are wounded by her desire to abandon him. In a more rational and detached moment, he recognizes that it would be both sensible and personally advantageous for him to sponsor her marriage to Junior: "Pues la verdad es que, pensándolo fríamente, a lo mejor no sería esa una mala salida, por mucho que a uno lo mortifique" [1057]. But in an actual confrontation with Candy, José Lino is incapable of either his imagined hauteur and totalitarian authority or his coldly calculated withdrawal. No matter how dispassionately he analyzes his position in writing, he cannot desist from trying to shape events to fit his self-image and immediate emotional needs. When confronted with Candy's antipathy he still does not desist from pursuing her, and only in retrospect does he gain the distance from himself to question his response: "¿Por qué tenía yo que humillarme, y soportarlo todo?" [1066].

While Candy's rejection of José Lino represents the culmination of an intensifying emotion, the real shock to his self-image comes with Corina's revelation that she has known that Candy accompanied him to Mexico almost since they left, ironically having read of it in his own words in a letter addressed to Candy's father. José Lino's assertions that no one fathomed his real motivation for disappearing, although he and Candy encountered Doménech in Mexico, or questioned the synchronism of his disappearance and reemergence with that of his secretary, are invalidated by this discovery as well as by Doménech's later actions. Never looking beyond Corina's knowledge, José Lino continues to rely on Doménech as a trustworthy and discreet friend in his attempt to win back Candy, whose nickname Doménech significantly coined for her in Mexico. Thus while Corina's revelation has considerably widened his limited narrative perspective, not José Lino but the reader benefits from the necessity of rethinking earlier impressions. Essentially José Lino's self-image is still too strong to allow him to view himself from the outside, as others see him.

José Lino never perceives the relationship between Corina and Rodríguez which blossomed in his absence, although he documents its rise and fall. In this, his narrative stance strongly parallels that of Henry M. Pulham,[5] the first-person narrator of J. P. Marquand's novel of the same title, which Romberg characterizes as presenting "an unusually striking example ... of indirect and unconscious in-

---

[5] *H. M. Pulham, Esquire* (Boston: Little, Brown, 1941).

formation."⁶ Romberg describes the narrator's self-projection in terms which could apply to José Lino's narration in Part I of *El fondo del vaso* as well, except as regards the narrator's high ideals which are replaced in José Lino's case by a naive opportunism contrasting with the calculated opportunism of others:

> He has a positive attitude to his fellow-men, but his knowledge of human nature is inadequate. His ideals are high, but the persons whom he idealizes are not so exalted as his ideals.... the climax of his whole story is the description of how his wife and his best friend commit adultery. All this, the reader of the novel is told — but the narrator gives the information without being aware that he is doing so; he is unaware of the facts, or rather, he does not understand what they signify.⁷

José Lino is hardly the positively drawn character which Henry Pulham is; his flaws are numerous and visible to the reader, and in a very limited way to himself, from the start of his narration. But while the implied authors' visions of humanity differ widely, the underlying narrative technique of unconscious self-revelation is strikingly similar in both novels. That is, the implied author communicates with the reader in an identical manner, through the reader's recognition of "the discrepancy between conscious direct information and unconscious indirect information." Romberg concludes in evaluating *H. M. Pulham*:

> as far as I know, there is no other first-person novel where this discrepancy is so thoroughly worked out all the way through the novel. It sets its imprint on the whole structure of Marquand's story, right from the description of the ideals and experiences of college years, up to his [Pulham's] unconscious portrayal of his wife's adultery with his best friend.⁸

This same discrepancy is maintained throughout Part I of *El fondo del vaso* and the first section of Part III, even after Corina has confessed her adultery, until José Lino begins to successfully draw

---

⁶ Romberg, p. 119.
⁷ Ibid.
⁸ Ibid., p. 120.

together the external and internal views of himself and formulate a conscious, direct self-presentation.

Like Henry Pulham, José Lino walks right in on a rendez-vous between his wife and his best friend, although the idea of adultery never crosses his mind as it briefly does Pulham's. Instead José Lino receives a clear warning in a dream, like the Biblical Joseph, "el otro José, el casto" [1091]. And whereas Pulham rejects the possibility of adultery immediately, José Lino fails to interpret the dream correctly. In it Don Cipriano Medrano discusses Doménech's marriage, observing that "su Doménech aguanta que la consorte le llame ladrón," continuing:

> en mi humilde opinión, fíjese bien lo que le digo, querido Ruiz, en mi opinión eso es muchísimo más grave, mucho más insufrible, que si, digamos, el gallego Rodríguez *le* pusiera los cuernos; pues, con los cuernos, *usted* puede enterarse, o no enterarse y hacerse el distraído, según prefiera; pero ¿cómo es posible no darse por enterado de un insulto lanzado así a la cara? [1090; emphasis added]

José Lino misinterprets the antecedent of the indirect object, assigning it to Doménech, since his name was last mentioned, concluding that Doménech is the cuckold. He also passes over the ambiguity of *usted,* here either the indefinite or a direct reference to José Lino. Don Medrano clearly sets forth the alternative for a cuckold, revealing what people believe José Lino's choice of responses to be. As Romberg points up with regard to Pulham, "subsequent negations [of the possibility of adultery] have on the reader an effect that is practically the opposite of what [Pulham] intends"; [9] similarly, José Lino's puzzlement over Don Medrano's warning only serves to underscore the message for the reader. While Romberg believes that *H. M. Pulham* constitutes an "utterly unique example" of the extent to which unconscious self-betrayal can be carried, [10] José Lino offers a more recent example of this technique of character presentation serving as the central narrative technique. Romberg summarizes the function of the narrator as follows:

---

[9] Ibid., p. 121.
[10] Ibid., p. 123.

> Thus the narrator's ignorance, or rather misunderstanding, of the facts that he communicates is the very mechanism of narrative technique employed by the author Marquand in this novel. The character of the narrator is the necessary condition making it possible for this device to succeed without turning the story into farce or rough satire; and the narrative device is also at the same time a means of explaining and illustrating the character of the narrator further.[11]

Unlike the narrator of *Muertes de perro*, José Lino Ruiz, as he unburdens himself on paper, is never in control of the image he projects either of himself or of others. Whereas the secondary narrators of *Muertes de perro* may reveal themselves to be distinct from Pinedo's presentation of them, in *El fondo del vaso* the narrator's very words reveal that all the characters, including himself, are different from the way he perceives them. Initially José Lino's perspective is severely limited by his self-confident unawareness of his own ignorance. Although he recognizes that others do not consider him overly intelligent, he confidently assumes himself to be more intelligent than they realize, whereas of course the reverse is true. In short, he lacks control over his own narrative. His unreliability as narrator lies in the distance between his self-image and the image the reader perceives through his words and actions, especially in his increasing self-justification as the pillars of his identity begin to crumble with Candy's desertion and Corina's revelation of her knowledge of the affair.

Despite the reader's dependence on José Lino's narration, since he is the sole narrator, the reader's knowledge is greater than the narrator's, creating a distance between them which varies with the degree of José Lino's self-awareness. When José Lino does give the reader access to another perspective than his own, by including the views and reactions of others, he does so unknowingly. Increasingly as he pours out his petty, self-serving story, José Lino comes to recognize the distance between his ideal self and his real self, as he fails repeatedly to project to others the image he holds of himself and as others fail to respond to the image he believes they should hold of him. Instead of facing up to this realization, he

---

[11] Ibid., p. 122.

escapes from it by taking to his bed with a convenient illness. When he believes himself to be determining events and manipulating reactions, it is evident to the reader that instead he is responding to the cues of others. His impulses are simple and direct, even when he characterizes them as devious; his assessment of others is elementary in attributing to them only the single, unencumbered response he desires to elicit. He works to achieve the immediate goal, without adequate attention to its ramifications. He accepts as truth only what he sees and hears, in the manner in which he interprets it; beyond that, nothing affects his image of the world. Despite a self-conscious awareness of certain limitations, he considers himself invulnerable, the master of his life. The tragedy is that he is unable to accept himself as he really is and to act accordingly; instead his self-respect disintegrates rapidly throughout Part I and this too is mirrored in his actions.

José Lino's retrospective presentation of the series of events culminating in the emotional state from which he makes each entry allows him to record both his intentions and the resultant response from a unified perspective. His demeanor in meetings with Candy, for example, never bears out his planned effect on her, and his evaluation of these encounters records his frustration with his own behavior. As he laments:

> Yo, que al planear esa entrevista [con Candy], tenía calculado mostrarme, por grados sucesivos, altivo, digno, magnánimo, dolido, quejoso, tierno, humilde, suplicante acaso, hasta ablandarle el corazón y revivir en él siquiera un eco de los sentimientos que... tuvo hacia mí, yo mismo eché a perder todo en un momento, y lo único que había conseguido era ofenderla más. [1101]

By referring to her relationship with Doménech, he has aroused her anger. In the context of his envisioned strategy, the remark has disastrous results:

> Cuando uno se va del seguro y se le dispara una tontería (que, a lo mejor, no es tan una tontería, pero resulta tonto haberla largado), cuando uno hace lo contrario de aquello que se había propuesto... lo más discreto sería abandonar el empeño y no hacer nada más. [1100]

From the perspective of the narrative present José Lino identifies both the rational course of action, which he did not follow, and the probable correctness of his unintended implications about Candy's relationship with her new boss. It is typical of José Lino that when, even unintentionally, he appraises a situation correctly, he must suffer humiliation. As he has observed earlier in discovering that unwittingly he has performed a great service for Don Cipriano Medrano in getting his candidate for Miss INCOLO elected, "La verdad es que nunca salen las cosas tan bien como cuando uno las hace sin darse cuenta" [1081]. While all of José Lino's planned actions go awry, purely by chance he occasionally hits upon the truth.

Corina, like Candy, Doménech and Rodríguez, fails to respond in accordance with José Lino's image of her, although he attributes the cause of this incomprehensible behavior to her "moods." He is continually thrown off balance by the responses of both Candy and Corina, especially by their lack of interest in the matters which preoccupy him most; his plans are foiled by the actions of Rodríguez and Doménech. In short, the complexities of human nature escape him: "¿Quién conoce al género humano?" [1041] he questions rhetorically, eliciting the reader's response that José Lino certainly does not. When unable to comprehend someone, José Lino rationalizes the actions as prompted by causes beyond those of which he is aware. For example, when Rodríguez verbally devours José Lino following his reference to Corina as "lo que constituye mi cotidiano menú" [1043], which Rodríguez perceives as a direct and public challenge, only José Lino cannot identify the motivation for Rodríguez's verbal attack. José Lino manifests only surprise and, assuming that the assembled crowd of friends shares his perspective, looks to them as witnesses to his disbelief, as he later records:

> ¡De veras que la gente es fantástica! Ante semejante andanada, yo me quedé como quien ve visiones. ¿Qué responde uno a una cosa así? Por toda respuesta, giré una mirada en torno, para que el mundo me fuera testigo de la insensatez en que puede caer un gallego borracho, y también para explicar tácitamente el digno silencio con que una persona que se encuentra en sus cabales acoge tales despropósitos. No hay que decirlo: todo el mundo estaba en ello; percibí ironía maliciosa en las pupilas de todos, y

> no faltó incluso quien, por echar leña al fuego, apuntara: "Hombre, Rodríguez, José Lino sabrá lo que se dice; déjelo usted que pondere su mercadería." [1044]

As is made explicit to the reader in José Lino's dream, his silence and lack of response to Rodríguez's affair with his wife is interpreted as tacit acceptance. Ignorant of Rodríguez's true interest in visiting his home, José Lino can only blithely record the public response, in the erroneous confidence that it is not directed toward him. The maliciously ironic glances he detects comment on his behavior, however, and not on Rodríguez's; the anonymous baiter adds fuels to the fire by ridiculing José Lino, not by taunting Rodríguez. José Lino is the one who neither "knows what he is talking about" nor what kind of "merchandise" his wife is. Far from supporting José Lino's perspective, the remark insults him; within the framework of his later dream, it becomes doubly ironic, since José Lino is not the consenting husband the speaker assumes.

On other occasions when faced with incomprehensible behavior, José Lino advances the theory of atmospheric influences, in much the same manner as Pinedo detected the hand of fate in the events he recorded. José Lino consciously subscribes to the pathetic fallacy, not as a literary device but as an explanatory device. As he details:

> (...digo "la atmósfera" porque, en efecto, parecería que ciertas alternativas del humor y disposición de ánimo de la gente no tienen otra causa, a veces, que la formación de una nube en el cielo, o el amago de una tormenta, o la persistencia del viento). [1039-40]

Removing responsibility from the human sphere, as does the invocation of fate, José Lino's reliance on the correspondence between human emotions and atmospheric conditions underscores the simplemindedness of his comprehension of the human being, and essentially relieves him of the burden of this comprehension.[12]

---

[12] As the critic Rodrigo Molina has observed of the role of "las fuerzas ocultas" — *la suerte, la casualidad, la fortuna, los cielos* — in *Muertes de perro*:

> para Ayala, como lo fue para Calderón, esas expresiones o términos tradicionales con que se trata de identificar la causa o factor determinante de los actos humanos libres y futuros contingentes, son

B. *Parts II and III*

Following José Lino's written narrative in Part I, a collection of newspaper clippings under the heading "El Caso del Junior R. a través de algunos recortes del diario capitalino 'El Comercio' " comprises Part II, tracing the investigation of Junior's murder from the events surrounding his death to the incarceration of José Lino Ruiz and the eventual determination of the latter's innocence. The reader, like the readers of the newspaper *El Comercio,* experiences the daily unfolding of evidence in the context of official police interpretation, transmitted at a consistent narrative distance of one day. A unified narrative perspective prevails throughout the articles, exhibiting a consistent bias and moral tone evident from the first in references to Luis R. Rodríguez as "nuestro querido compañero de redacción" [1103] and later in the rivalry between newspapers for primacy in news reporting. The series of daily articles presents a collective but personified view of events, often employing the editorial "we," with the newspaper's self-image the dominant factor in the narrative focus. At least one critic has characterized the news reporting of Part II as "un recuento de hechos de apariencia objetiva que nos van revelando lo ocurrido," [13] in an apparent confusion between the absence of an identified first-person narrator ("who is nonetheless implicit in the collective "we") and objectivity. Whether individual or collective, the perspective is necessarily — and here blatantly as well — subjective, limited and only one of an infinite number of possible perspectives. The intent is never to achieve objectivity; the narrative technique adds a new and divergent perspective on the personalities of José Lino's narrative. Representing one component of the press, specifically the newspaper for which Rodríguez writes, out of the total Establishment structure, the clippings provide a distanced perspective on José Lino

---

fórmula o recurso poético si se quiere, de que se valen estos autores para comunicar la realidad de las limitaciones humanas.

"*Muertes de perro*: Triple dimensión" in *Estudios* (Madrid: Insula, 1961), p. 22.

[13] Jorge Enjuto, "Francisco Ayala: *El fondo del vaso,*" *Asomante,* 20 (1964), 82.

while at the same time casting Rodríguez in a new light by focusing on his son.

As will be recalled, both Pinedo and the Spanish Ambassador recognized the importance of newspaper accounts as secondary sources in their narrative reconstruction of events. In the fictional introduction forming part of the section "Recortes del diario *Las Noticias,* de ayer" of Francisco Ayala's recent collection *El jardín de las delicias,* the first-person narrator-editor explains that he has gathered the clippings which follow "buscando usar la prensa diaria como espejo del mundo en que vivimos."[14] The clippings forming Part II of *El fondo del vaso* serve this same function of mirroring society, encompassing in their coverage social movements (gang warfare, spiritual religions, youth culture) and institutions (newspaper journalism, police, justice).

For the first time the reader views José Lino wholly from an external perspective, a mirror in which the José Lino of Part I is grotesquely and publicly deformed, the defects in his character distorted as in a caricature. His strictness as an employer, in which he took much pride, is upheld by the newspaper — " '[don José Lino], cuya fama de patrón estricto está muy extendida en los medios comerciales' " [1118] — but to his detriment, since it makes his relationship with Candy all the more singular. Initially the newspaper depicts José Lino as a prominent businessman, " 'una personalidad no carente de relieve y generalmente apreciada en nuestros ambientes sociales' " [1117]. Later when the bankruptcy of Casa Ruiz occurs with José Lino helpless in jail, the newspaper comments:

> "En la quiebra de dicho negocio puede verse simbolizada la más completa quiebra moral de su dueño.... Quienes ingenuamente trataban, consideraban y estimaban a Ruiz como un miembro honorable de nuestra comunidad, hallarán ocasión de nueva sorpresa y de gran escándalo en ciertos detalles curiosos..., poniendo al descubierto que los fundamentos éticos del sujeto en cuestión eran tal falsos, tan deleznables, como la base económica de su empresa mercantil." [1127-28]

---

[14] (Barcelona: Seix Barral, 1971), p. 16.

Here the collective voice of the newspaper functions as a Greek chorus expressing society's public, hypocritical response to the public revelation of José Lino's sexploitation of Candy. José Lino himself provides the reader with a foretaste of society's response to moral transgressions in recording that Rodríguez had once been caught in a blackmail scandal, "de la que no logró salir sin trabajo y pública rechifla" [1056]. At the time José Lino remarks prematurely, in reference to his relationship with Candy: "Yo, por mi parte, he sido mucho más afortunado."

Knowing what he does about José Lino, the reader envisions his responses to the disastrous turn of events from the newspaper accounts of his behavior. It becomes apparent that José Lino was less than candid in his last entry in Part I, written several days after Junior's death, to which he refers, as he lies confined to his bed by an illness, the origin of which he suspiciously traces to the day of his humiliating encounter with Candy at Doménech's bank, and to which he succumbed upon receiving the news of Junior's death. As the net draws tighter around him, building from the circumstantial evidence of a note he sent to Junior on the day of the latter's death, José Lino's illness clearly becomes an emotional response to a situation he cannot face; it represents his attempt to escape from the tangled web in which he is by now tightly bound by his own incriminating if criminally innocent actions, compounded in turn by his denials of fact. Rather than admit publicly to his relationship with Candy, of which he was once so proud, he attempts to physically absent himself from the picture through illness. This childish response arouses little reader sympathy for José Lino, despite his predicament and the reader's assumption of his innocence, but instead places him in a grotesque light.

Part III of *El fondo del vaso* returns to José Lino's first-person perspective, but not in a written narrative with its implicit distance from the events narrated, however minimal. Imprisoned on a charge of murder, his business empire in shambles and the details of his personal life thrown open to all, José Lino whiles away the hours by meditating on his life. The result is a conscious, coherent narration which, on the narrative plane, yields no distance between thought or emotion and the mental recording of it, but which on the action plane encompasses the entire spectrum of José Lino's life and projects into the future as well, exactly as in the written narrative. In Part I José Lino has followed Rodríguez's advice to write as he speaks:

> Yo me puse a la obra aplicando la receta que el mismo Rodríguez me había dado: "Lo que tienes que hacer es escribir aquellas mismas palabras y frases que dirías si quisieras expresarte verbalmente. También cuando uno habla, la conversación diaria arrastra cantidad enorme de materiales literarios. No hay sino ponerlo, negro sobre blanco, en el papel: tal es el secreto, y no otro." [1045-46]

This similarity of construction justifies the similarity of narrative style between the notebook entries and the inner monologue of Part III, although the latter contains some exclusively oral constructions as well. When the narrative plane and the action (mental, in this case) plane coincide, eliminating the narrative distance inherent in all other narrative forms, José Lino's narrative reproduces a disconnected series of thoughts, the broken flow of discovery, as in the following example:

> O ¿no pudiera ser que...? A menos que... Sí, ahora lo veo; ahora caigo en ello. Sí, ya está; eso ha de ser: eso lo explica todo. ¿Cómo no lo había pensado antes? Cuando uno está empachado, si vuelve a cargar el estómago de nuevo, entonces es cuando ya no tiene medio de contenerse... ¿No será que Corina...? [1159]

Before returning to his more familiar style, José Lino has narrated on a purely verbal level, which cannot be imagined in a written record.

In line with Rodríguez's observations on the rhetorical nature of speech as well as of writing, José Lino is conscious of the structuring his thoughts undergo even before he utters them. This imposed structure distances him from their content, although no narrative distance as such exists. José Lino's meditation on the narrative act justifies both the impossibility of a written narrative and the verbal format of his oral narrative, predisposing the reader to accept his hackneyed portrayal of emotions as consistent with his character revealed in Part I:

> Sí; para encajar dentro de formas legibles las agradables sutilezas de la divagación insensata, uno tiene que falsifi-

> carlas: la retórica se le impone. Pero quizás la retórica sea de todas maneras ineludible para mí.... Lo cierto es que, anterior incluso a la palabra escrita, se filtra hasta en las lucubraciones enfáticas del desdichado preso, que sólo a través de palabras consigue pensar. Así, cavilando, *compone*. Eso es: compone. ¿Hay acaso retórico mayor, por otra parte, que el sentimiento mismo? Cuanto más sincero y hondo, más retórico.... Procuraré, pues, analizar *in mente* ... [1146]

Distinct from the interior monologue, José Lino's monologue is analytical in nature. Since it occurs after his initial reaction to Corina's confession of her infidelity and after the initial trauma of imprisonment has worn away, José Lino stands at some distance, both temporally and emotionally, from the central concern of his thoughts. After establishing his narrative perspective, José Lino moves chronologically through his prison experience to his present emotional state. Spanning less than twenty-four hours, the two chapters of his monologue, separated by a dream-filled sleep, form a unity of focus and development. Now truly alone, as symbolized by his physical isolation, he dialogues with himself, offering a multiplicity of hypothetical explanations for Corina's behavior before coming to grips with himself at the end. Indeed, at times he addresses himself by name, as the rational self comes into conflict with the emotional, escapist self:

> Basta, basta. No caigamos en el absurdo, otra vez, ahora por la banda opuesta. No deliremos de nuevo. ¡Ay, José Lino, qué trabajo te cuesta aceptar la amarga realidad, tragar la píldora! ... Pero, hijo mío, hay que tragársela, qué remedio. No nos engañemos, ahora a sabiendas. Dejemos los actos de santidad para los santos. [1171]

Despite his early warning to himself that he keep a clear head and not become incoherent — "Cuidado, pues; mucho cuidado: no pierdas la cabeza, no desvaríes, José Lino" [1146] — only at the end of his train of thought in the first chapter does he strike off into an irrational explanation of Corina's action. The dream brings reconciliation to his present condition. Searching the depths of his being, in a union of his two selves which signals his new self-awareness and the resolution of the distance between his self-image and the image others hold of him, José Lino ultimately comes to share the responsibility for his fate with Corina. The time differential between Parts I and III, as well as the intervening perspective of Part II, prepare for the change which José Lino has undergone, leading the reader to accept his new introspection and self-awareness. José Lino himself compares his emotional response in Part I and in the unrecorded days which follow his response to the news of his bankruptcy, noting the calmness and detachment of his state of mind from the isolation of a prison cell:

> yo que había tomado como un terrible agravio las molestias, al fin pasajeras, de esta detención (para no hablar — antes — de las pamplinas de Candy, que me sacaron de quicio), ahora en cambio, tras de madurar no sé por cuánto tiempo en este calabozo, recibí con una cierta dosis de filosofía la noticia de la catástrofe que desbarata mi vida entera y me hace polvo, que me ha reducido a la indigencia, dejándome tirado en la vía, donde mi buen nombre de comerciante honrado se arrastra. [1153]

This absence of emotion with which José Lino recounts his misfortunes distances the reader as well from the events.

Bertil Romberg is concerned with establishing the epic situation of such narratives as José Lino's in Part III, narratives which are entirely in the form of what he terms "interior monologue." [15] As Romberg writes of Arthur Schnitzler's *Leutnant Gustl*:

---

[15] Several critics have characterized Part III of *El fondo del vaso* as *monólogo interior,* among them Keith Ellis, *Arte narrativo,* p. 223, and Andrés Amorós, "Prólogo" to Ayala, *Obras narrativas completas,* p. 78. However, Robert Humphrey has established a somewhat limited definition of interior monologue with which José Lino's monologue does not coincide:

> Interior monologue is, then, the technique used in fiction for representing the psychic *content and processes* of character, partly or entirely unuttered, just as these processes exist at various levels of conscious control before they are formulated for deliberate speech. [emphasis added]

Stream of Consciousness in the Modern Novel (Berkeley: Univ. of California Press, 1954), p. 24. Humphrey further clarifies that interior monologue "is not presented, formally, for the information of the reader"; pp. 26-27. José Lino's monologue retains "conventional syntax and diction" throughout — hence its structural similarity to Part I — and suggests "mental wandering" only through its content, never its form; p. 26.

Following Humphrey's definition, Part III belongs to the pre-stream-of-consciousness category, like Robert Penn Warren's *All the King's Men* (New

the main character depicts in an interior monologue the experiences and reflections of a night. The narrative is not *written* by the narrator, nor has he any audience for whom he is narrating; instead, the narrative is expressed in the thoughts and reflections of the narrator. The term "thinking aloud" inevitably occurs to one when one attempts to define Lieutenant Gustl's story, although one may go no farther than to call it a disciplined and carefully arranged form of interior monologue, which points forward to the stream of consciousness method.... The monologue is carried out as the first-person narrator wanders about a [sic] night in the streets of Vienna. But can one really speak of an epic situation in this story at all? [16]

Since the identification of the epic situation is fundamental to Romberg's definition of the first-person novel, he requires a credible connection between the narrative content and the process of communicating it to the reader, whether in writing or orally. His critique applies equally to Part III of *El fondo del vaso,* except that within the confines of his prison cell José Lino is necessarily limited to mental action. Romberg concludes in reference to the impact of this narrative technique on the reader:

> The lieutenant's story is a piece of direct, and above all indirect, self-analysis, which is highly private in nature. It is conceived and experienced by the narrator, but it simply *cannot* be thought of as being communicated by the narrator himself. It is clear that the author has fixed his point of view in the consciousness of the narrator, and it is likewise clear that in the characterization of the narrator he infallibly contains himself within the limits of

---

York: Harcourt, Brace, 1946). Both novels present "fundamentally a study of moral development and ethical awakening in the central character" through "an inner drama of consciousness"; pp. 114-15. Both authors offer a naturalistic rendering of the inner world through the use of rhetoric, symbols, concrete images and, to a lesser extent in Ayala, free association, rather than the impressionistic rendering which characterizes stream of consciousness; pp. 113-16. Since Humphrey attaches no label to this naturalistic method, this study refers to José Lino's monologue in Part III of *El fondo del vaso* as an "inner monologue," to distinguish it from the interior monologue, following the usage of Brian T. Fitch in "Aesthetic Distance and Inner Space in the Novels of Camus," *Modern Fiction Studies,* 10 (1964), 281.

[16] Romberg, p. 99; Arthur Schnitzler, "*None But the Brave*" [Trans. of *Leutnant Gustl*], trans. Richard L. Simon, in *Viennese Novelettes* (New York: Simon and Schuster, 1925), pp. 393-433.

this consciousness. And yet the [implied] author is detected behind the narrator! However earnestly we summon to our aid the willing suspension of disbelief, Lieutenant Gustl's experiences cannot be narrated and communicated to the reader by any other person than a [implied] author.[17]

However, Romberg does not limit this condemnation of authorial intrusion merely to Schnitzler, but includes the later stream of consciousness novels as a whole, thus invalidating his criticism for readers who accept the stream of consciousness technique without question. Although his distinction between stream of consciousness novels and the "autonomous first-person novel" holds, Romberg has made the question of authority the central test for inclusion in his study of the first-person novel.

By Romberg's definition then, neither *Muertes de perro* nor *El fondo del vaso* is an autonomous first-person novel. While the epic situation of both the first novel and Part I of the second could "conceivably enable the narrator to make contact with readers or audience,"[18] the manner in which this contact is made is never specified. The narrative perspectives of both novels uphold the validity of Romberg's contention that:

> modern narrative prose has to a great extent departed from the issue of authority and no longer shows such an ardent solicitude to verify its facts for the sake of the illusion of reality; but has deepened and brought into sharper focus the study of the mind or minds which form the centre in the story.[19]

As Romberg acknowledges, the focus of concern has shifted away from external, editorial justification for the existence of a narrative. In the modern Spanish novel this shift can be exemplified by the differing roles the reader assumes in *Pascual Duarte* or *Pabellón de reposo*, with their inclusion of external and internal authority for the written narratives, and in *Tiempo de silencio* or *Señas de identidad*, with only internal authority and the use of interior monologue replacing written narrative.

---

[17] Ibid., pp. 99-100.
[18] Ibid., p. 100.
[19] Ibid.

In short, Francisco Ayala has chosen to eliminate the distance as well as the authority of an editorial voice, requiring the reader to rely directly and exclusively on the narrator. Pinedo and José Lino carry the full burden of convincing the reader of the verisimilitude of their narratives, whether written or oral in origin, and positioning him into the willing suspension of disbelief. Not the player of a game who must pass through a series of frames external to the narrative before reaching it directly, the reader of Ayala's novels enters immediately into direct contact with the primary narrator who shoulders the burden of establishing a convincing communication. Since the reader is not being asked to accept the isolated autonomy of the narrative world, he stands both within and outside of the narration, an ambiguous position which allows him to approach the narrative directly and yet to draw the vision of mankind it projects into his own life.

The external structure of *El fondo del vaso,* like the title of *Muertes de perro,* lies outside the narrator's original manuscript. The unique composition of each part, the division into chapters, the titles — all this is superimposed on José Lino's written and oral narratives. Unlike the earlier novel, which contains no chapter titles and in which the division into chapters can be shown to reveal Pinedo's hand, *El fondo del vaso* with its composite structure confronts the reader with a continual reminder of a presence superceding the narrator's. Whereas the chapter headings of Part I and the titles of Parts II and III offer summations of the contents or situate the narrative, the two chapter headings of Part III establish an ironic commentary on José Lino's monologue which serves to distance the reader before he can begin to read it. Both chapter titles in Part III derive from José Lino's monologue. The first revives the association with *carambolas* which Pinedo made famous in his epitaph of José Lino, murdered for "sus ufanas series de interminables carambolas" [862]. José Lino employs *carambola* metaphorically, in referring to Corina's latest move, her confession, to raise the crucial question of motivation: "faltaría decidir si el último golpe de la carambola no habrá sido obra del azar antes que del cálculo" [1163]. The chapter heading, "La gran carambola," broadens the application of this metaphor to refer to the blow which has felled both José Lino and Corina herself. Lodged ironically enough in "la cárcel del Miserere," José Lino receives Corina's appeal for pardon impassively, only coming to recognize at the end of his monologue that he should have pardoned her and in turn requested her pardon. The title of the second chapter puns on the word *gracia* in the sense of pardon, either human or, in the context of the Miserere, divine. José Lino's combination of "triste gracia" is ironic in itself, while again the chapter title, "La triste gracia" broadens the application to reflect both his and Corina's fate. Additionally, the phrase popularly refers to "something unpleasant."

In his monologue José Lino attributes to Corina the assessment of himself that " 'Ha hecho muchas cosas que no debiera, *pero en el fondo* no es tan malo; *en el fondo,* es bueno," [1169; emphasis added]. The title *El fondo del vaso* characterizes the narrative posture of José Lino in Part III when, after his cup of life has been drained to the bottom drop, he engages in a soul searching reaching to the depths of his being. Ayala himself has clarified the relationship between José Lino's emotional state and the novel's title in describing the narrator: "el protagonista, rota la falaz tela de araña de las relaciones sociales que a todos nos sostienen, cae, *toca fondo* y, en la soledad, se encuentra por fin a sí mismo clamando misericordia."[20] But the expression itself has roots in *Muertes de perro,* in which Pinedo's Aunt Loreto employs it in a conversation with her nephew. From her privileged perspective as former companion to Doña Concha, Loreto makes an assertion which she then refuses to clarify for Pinedo, in discussing with him Bocanegra's reaction to Doña Concha's affair with Tadeo:

> — Bocanegra no sabía nada — me contestó [Loreto] —, ni tampoco quería saber nada. Al final, lo único que le interesaba a Bocanegra era el fondo del vaso. Y otros — añadió con una sonrisa enigmática. [947]

Within the context of Loreto's remark, the phrase "el fondo del vaso" refers on the primary level to Bocanegra's propensity to drink himself nightly into a stupor, while the zeugmatic construction *otros* introduces the economic dimension of the plural *fondos* [funds, resources]. Although Pinedo asserts, "Creo que no era, desde luego, a dinero a lo que aludía [Loreto] con estos otros

---

[20] Ayala, *Mis mejores páginas,* p. 261; emphasis added.

fondos" [947], money certainly constitutes a secondary level of interpretation substantiated elsewhere in the novel. Both Doménech's fall from favor and fortune, reversed in *El fondo del vaso,* and Luis Rosales' suicide, appear to result from Bocanegra's desire to maneuver himself into control of their property.[21] Finances occupy an even more prominent position in the second novel: economic prosperity reigns. The Medrano empire, the prominent financial positions occupied by the formerly "dead" José Lino and the once ruined Doménech — all attest to the propitious atmosphere for economic gain under the new regime. But in *El fondo del vaso* the economic overtones linking the two novels through the title of the second yield to a different sort of *fondo,* the depths of human character.[22]

---

[21] When reading Pinedo's rejection of a possible reference to finances in Loreto's cryptic "y otros," the reader has not yet encountered the Spanish Minister's account of Luis Rosales' economic situation at the time of his suicide, which provides an additional perspective on Loreto's view of Bocanegra's greed:

> Cuando [Luis Rosales] aceptó entrar al servicio de su régimen... esperaba, y tal vez se le prometió expresa o tácitamente, que los bienes de [su hermano el senador Lucas Rosales], hallándose expatriados como lo estaban su viuda e hijos, pasarían a poder suyo mediante algún truco judicial o administrativo, pues la conducta del senador Rosales se encontraba sometida, *post mortem,* a procedimientos de investigación en los cuales quedaba embargada su fortuna para responder de posibles cargos. De hecho, no solo habían sido, al final, definitivamente confiscadas esas propiedades... sino que ahora ya Bocanegra no necesitaba más de [Luis Rosales]. [958]

[22] On this metaphorical level, the expression "el fondo del vaso" evokes the exchange in *Luces de Bohemia* between the poet Max Estrella and Don Latino de Hispalis following Max's assertion that: "El sentido trágico de la vida española sólo puede darse con una estética sistemáticamente deformada."

> Max.—...La deformación deja de serlo cuando está sujeta a una matemática perfecta. Mi estética actual es transformar con matemática de espejo cóncavo las normas clásicas.
> Don Latino.—¿Y dónde está el espejo?
> Max.—En el fondo del vaso.
> ... ...
> Latino, deformemos la expresión en el mismo espejo que nos deforma las caras y toda la vida miserable de España.

Ramón María del Valle-Inclán, *Luces de Bohemia* (1924; rpt. Madrid: Espasa-Calpe, 1961), pp. 106-07.

In Ayala's two novels, the narrators' own worldviews communicate to the reader a deformed vision of human life (made explicit in the title *Muertes de perro*) in modern society. Part II of *El fondo del vaso* with its broad satire

The reader of *El fondo del vaso* initially views José Lino from the distance which Rodríguez's tone in the opening paragraph and the references to Pinedo's manuscript interpose. As José Lino's perspective prevails, the reader recognizes the narrator's limitations which keep open the distance between them. However, José Lino's ingenuousness, his obvious lack of malice and the inherent simplicity of the emotional responses make him an essentially sympathetic narrator. Even his pride and blinding self-image are so misguided as to arouse sympathy. Although his interpretation of events is limited by his comprehension of them, making him unreliable on this level, José Lino's narrative remains a reliable record of what he sees and hears. Despite his past actions, in the narrative present José Lino holds the reader at his side; victimized by his "friends" and wife, José Lino remains deaf to the malicious remarks which encompass him. Recoiling from the society in which José Lino moves, its corrupted values symbolized by Don Cipriano Medrano, the reader has only José Lino's perspective with which to sympathize.

The reader's greater comprehension, his ability to interpret what José Lino records and detect the implied author's ironic hand, places him on a superior plane to the narrator. The numerous references to José Lino's simplemindedness or stupidity underscore this distance between reader and narrator. Similarly, the other characters' lack of respect for José Lino heightens the reader's sense of superiority. Thus the reader's sympathy for the narrator does not bring him to identify himself with José Lino; the distance between them remains too great. Instead, the reader's sympathy is directed toward a human being suffering from the frailties of human nature. Aware of the self-destruction toward which his vanity is leading him, and despite his moments of lucid self-appraisal, José Lino lacks the strength of character to let Candy leave him for Junior;

---

of society looming behind the journalist's columns most strongly suggests the systematic deformation of society as though viewed through a concave lens, as Max Estrella describes. While Ayala's fiction is most often compared with that of Cervantes, Quevedo or even Galdós, critics have also frequently cited the comparison with Valle-Inclán, especially in an attempt to find a common subject in Valle-Inclán's *Tirano Banderas* and Ayala's *Muertes de perro*. The most that one can say here is that both authors evoke the expression "el fondo del vaso" to stress the vision of the human character which each seeks to present in his own way.

his self-image will not permit it. This is the struggle with which the reader identifies. Only when at the end of Part I he takes to his bed does José Lino cut a ridiculous figure in the reader's eyes, but the reader does not recognize this fully until Part II where he views José Lino from a distanced perspective; at the time, José Lino's withdrawal seems more pathetic.

From the newspaper articles in Part II it becomes clear to the reader that José Lino is also the unwitting victim of the collective voice of society, its institutions, as his unjust incarceration and bankruptcy make symbolically clear. In a different context, a critic has described the response to the man unjustly accused of murder, citing:

> la sympathie que nous éprouvons tous pour celui qui fait figure de victime de la société, pour l'individu confronté et persécuté par une société hostile qui ne le comprend pas. C'est une situation classique que le lecteur reconnaît au premier coup d'œil et sa sympathie va instinctivement au plus faible, comme le romancier l'avait bien prévu en choisissant une réplique moderne du conflit romantique entre individu et société: l'erreur judiciaire, un danger parmi bien d'autres qui menacent l'homme de l'époque bureaucratique et totalitaire.[23]

José Lino is the unheroic victim in modern society, but at the same time it remains clear to the reader that José Lino shares the responsibility for his plight through his failure to admit the truth either to himself or to the officials. The newspaper account of José Lino's behavior after Junior's death serves to distance the reader at the very moment in which the situation itself calls for the greatest sympathy, preparing the distance between reader and narrator at the start of Part III and additionally eliminating all possibility of pity. As José Lino eventually comes to recognize: "cada cual lleva dentro de sí mismo a su peor enemigo" [1168]. While his unfaithfulness to Corina structurally requires punishment, the catastrophe which befalls him does not constitute poetic, but rather satiric, justice. Schematically, Corina's unfaithfulness, rooted in

---

[23] Brian T. Fitch, *Narrateur et Narration dans "L'Etranger" d'Albert Camus, Analyse d'un fait littéraire*, 2nd ed., Les Archives des Lettres Modernes, No. 34 (Paris: Lettres Modernes, 1968), p. 157.

EL FONDO DEL VASO 109

José Lino's absence in Mexico, serves as his punishment and her vindication, equilibrating their respective situations. Ironically, society does not punish their behavior as much as José Lino's indiscretion, his failure to conceal his behavior from society.

Despite the sympathy inherent in José Lino's situation, including the timing of Corina's confession to him, his initial self-centered, self-serving explanations of Corina's actions only diminish this sympathy; he blames Corina, seeing himself as the innocent victim. In the context of his "loss of honor," José Lino projects himself as a Christ figure in a series of references — "el árbol de esta cruz," "inri," and describing Corina: "viene a hacérseme arrepentida Magdalena" [1147] — culminating in his casting himself as the crucified Christ:

> Quien ... se encuentra hoy en la cárcel bajo concepto de asesino, ha sufrido un expolio que lo deja en cueros, y sobre su cabeza exhibe, para universal befa y ludibrio, el cartelito infame de los maridos burlados. ¡Tan cierto es que del árbol caído todos hacen leña! Sí, pues leña, palos, bofetadas, escupitajos: *Ecce homo.* [1147-48] [24]

The incongruity of the traditional concept of honor and Christ's passion signals the gross incompatibility of José Lino's projection of himself as the sacrificial victim with the reality of the circumstances. Indeed, the very use of the imagery alienates the reader.

When after awakening from his sleep, José Lino for the first time begins to see himself clearly and accept himself as he is, the distance separating him from the reader narrows. In addition the elimination of narrative distance throughout most of this last chapter brings the reader into the greatest direct contact with José Lino. Stepping outside himself in an attempt to view the situation as Corina must have, José Lino ceases to stand at the center of his own narration. With an understanding of Corina's visit to the prison, he finally accepts his share of the guilt, but ironically, his realization comes too late; both remain alone and unforgiven. After

---

[24] Here José Lino alludes to society's treatment of him, drawing upon the proverb introduced in reference to Bocanegra, when José Lino, following Rodríguez's argument, contends that the publishers of *Muertes de perro* sought to "dar pábulo a la común malignidad que siempre hace leña del árbol caído" [1028].

standing above José Lino throughout most of *El fondo del vaso,* the reader begins to identify with him, as his awareness merges with the reader's superior knowledge at the close of the monologue. Yet this identification is never complete, since the reader is aware throughout Part III that José Lino has lost his opportunity to accept Corina's confession and in turn receive her pardon. Only when he realizes this, does he discover how truly alone he is. This constant irony distances the reader from the subject of the monologue, even though in other respects he shares the narrator's perspective.

As in *Muertes de perro,* the implied author of *El fondo del vaso* offers no moral judgment; man is both innocent and guilty. José Lino's closing words to himself demonstrate the position of the implied author towards the characters, a position which incorporates both sympathy and the more distant pity, both identification and superiority:

> Tuvo que marcharse [Corina], otra vez con el fardo de su Desliz a cuestas, y me dejó solo (¿no era eso, acaso, lo que tan orgullosamente procuré siempre yo?); solo para siempre, solo y pataleando en el fango. ¡Que Dios nos ampare! [1176]

Thus the novel closes with the Miserere. The vision of mankind "pataleando en el fango" strongly resembles the imagery of *Muertes de perro* reducing man to a sub-human level and contrasts sharply with José Lino's overriding sense of pride at the narration's start.

CHAPTER IV

IMPLIED AUTHOR AND READER COMMUNICATE

Having examined the narrative presence in Francisco Ayala's two novels, it is now time to shift the focus to a consideration of the manner in which the implied author communicates with the reader either through or over the head of the narrator. Indications have already been established that in each novel the reader remains largely distanced from the narrator, although the narrative personalities reveal themselves in dissimilar manners. This distance, which shifts at the close of each narrative, derives from the reader's response to the narrative personality as well as from his assessment of the degree to which the narrator voices the norms of the implied author. Since Pinedo has been characterized as an unreliable narrator and José Lino as unreliable on the conscious level, the reader must seek the implied author's stance in the ironic distance between the narrator's interpretation of the words and actions he records and the reader's own evaluation of them. While the broad scope of the irony present in the two novels has been indicated in the preceding chapters, the question of the role of irony in the communication process remains unexamined.

As a self-conscious, detached narrator throughout all but the last pages of his narrative, excepting in his relationship with Olóriz, Pinedo engages in a certain amount of incidental verbal irony. Indeed, he acknowledges the ironist in himself [951], although he is repulsed by the same ironic distance attained by Tadeo Requena [901]. For example, Pinedo responds ironically to Sobrarbe's confession that he salvaged the pages of Tadeo Requena's diary: "—Con los demás recuerditos de Tadeo —completé yo, sonriendo"

[1006]. Pinedo's ironic observation, based on an implicit view of human nature, rings truer than even he imagines, as Sobrarbe's confession reveals that the *recuerditos* include Tadeo's entire savings. In this manner Pinedo's original overt irony becomes genuine understatement, as the ironist's ignorance of the situation he ironizes is unmasked. The response elicited by Pinedo's ironic observation is duplicated later by Pinedo's own reaction to Olóriz's probing into the source of Pinedo's sudden wealth. In this larger context, Pinedo becomes the victim of a dramatized irony instead of the ironist, as the implied author's vision of mankind includes Pinedo in its scope.

Pinedo frequently engages in ironic understatement in his narrative commentary, as when he observes of Camarasa's article, "Cómo se hace una nación":

> Este artículo fue en su día objeto de un pequeño escándalo, un mero escandalete, sin consecuencias; digo, sin consecuencias inmediatas, porque remotas había de tenerlas, y muy graves, irreparables, para su autor. [915]

After first down-playing the importance of the event from *escándalo* to *escandalete,* Pinedo reverses his perspective and augments the impact to *graves, irreparables.* These understated *consecuencias* to which Pinedo alludes in a leap from a contemporary viewpoint to the superior knowledge of the narrative present consist of course of Camarasa's death, as the reader will learn. In contrast, the double entendre of the proverb, "madrugar es sano, ya me lo decía la abuela" [1017], which Pinedo smugly cites following the description of his early-morning murder of Olóriz, is readily transparent to the reader. While the action may appear *sano* to Pinedo in his enthusiasm, it certainly has not been a healthy experience for Olóriz, nor will it prove so in the long run for Pinedo. Through this ironic understatement of his emotions, Pinedo verbalizes his blindness to the future consequences for himself; the detached reader who at this point stands at his farthest from Pinedo places the remark in a larger ironic context, a context in which Pinedo again becomes the object of the covert irony and no longer the overt ironist.

The manner in which Pinedo draws the reader's attention to the multiple ironies in the circumstances surrounding Doña Concha's death exemplifies his role as a covert ironist in the larger context of direct implied author-reader communication. In informing the reader that Doña Concha died in the Inmaculada prison, Pinedo merely juxtaposes, but does not comment upon, the fact that both bear the same name, a name which in the context of Doña Concha's activity in (and out of) prison is ironic indeed:

> la inefable doña Concha, a quien centenares, quizás, de voluntarios, allá en el chiquero-prisión de la Inmaculada, pasaron por las armas (con este eufemismo canalla se lo significaba, guiñando el ojo) antes de que un sádico imbécil pusiera término al general entretenimiento machacándole el cráneo. La ilustre matrona se había labrado con su conducta un final tan lamentable, hasta el punto de que algunos pudieran considerarlo merecido castigo. [863]

Pinedo's ironic phraseology, inappropriate in tone to the situation described, underscores the opposition between Immaculate Conception and Doña Concha's legendary promiscuity, as does his reference to the prison as a *chiquero* [bullpen]. The contrast in tone between his detached description of her life as creating "general entretenimiento" and the brutal description of the manner in which she died, signals the change in viewpoint from disassociation to a moral context. In ascribing the military imagery to the collective voice of society, Pinedo detaches himself from this vision, which he terms *canalla,* as he further does by indicating that Doña Concha's demise was considered just punishment. His original overt irony becomes genuine understatement, as the ironist's ignorance of the situation he ironizes is unmasked. By the presentation of her death from this distanced, hostile view, Pinedo shapes the reader's response, pointing up the ironies.

The use of literary and historical allusions also contributes to the ironic dimension of Pinedo's narrative. In referring to Tadeo Requena's response to Doña Concha's advances, Pinedo remarks that Tadeo is "fiel a su táctica cazurra de vergonzoso en Palacio" [929], ironically comparing Tadeo's unwilling correspondence with that of the hero of Tirso de Molina's play of the same title. The irony derives from the distance between the two situations, not to mention their outcome, which the differing connotations of *vergonzoso* underscore. Tadeo is not only timid but shamed by his capitulation to his lover's designs; Tirso's hero is merely timid. By reference to the play, Pinedo highlights the illicit nature of the relationship between Bocanegra's wife and an unknown, probably his illegitimate son, as well as contrasting Tadeo's presentation of his helpless response with that of a true *vergonzoso*.[1]

Overriding the distinction which has been maintained between the conscious verbal irony in which both Pinedo and Tadeo Requena engage, and situational irony which may be ascribed to the narrator or to the implied author, depending on the narrator's distance from the situation, as seen above, on the structural level all irony is assignable to the implied author. Insofar as the narrator serves as the conscious vehicle for transmitting the irony to the reader, his voice coincides with that of the implied author. But much of the irony functions on a level beyond the narrator's scope of awareness. For example, the characters remain unaware of the ironies inherent in proper names, since these constitute the reality of their world. Not only the names of Doña Concha, already discussed, or of Bocanegra, on which Ayala himself has commented, or the more obvious Ángelo, but the place name San Cosme contain an ironic dimension. In ironic support of the allusion to the patron saint of physicians, the town is famous for a certain "brutal operación quirúrgica" [881], as the Spanish Minister delicately terms castration, practiced on several of its residents at different times.

On a structural level the novel displays an ironic attitude towards the working of fate, an attitude which Pinedo only in part verbalizes. In ironic reversal, fate seems to punish "success," as the protagonist conceives it, in a consistent display of divine retribution; witness Pancho Cortina's literal descent from a position of power upon which Pinedo comments. Pinedo sets the course for the reader's awareness of this irony of fate by highlighting the contrast between narrative perspectives. Early in his narrative he remarks on the ironic truth of the observations on fate with which Tadeo opens his diary:

> tú mismo ignorabas hasta qué punto es imprevisible el curso de la humana existencia, y qué tremenda verdad en-

---

[1] Hiriart also discusses this allusion to Tirso's play in *Las alusiones literarias*, pp. 79-80.

cerraban las frases y artificios de literato aficionado con
que diste comienzo a tus memorias... [867]

The irony is compounded for the reader by his knowledge that Pinedo remains as blind to his fate as does Tadeo to his; in fact, in a retrospective consideration of the novel, the reader possesses the same foreknowledge of Pinedo's fate as Pinedo does of Tadeo's in writing his manuscript. Tadeo philosophizes on Doménech's rapid descent from Director of the Banco Nacional to a prison cell in the following terms: " ¡Ah, si la gente supiera observar, muchas sorpresas no serían tales, y más de uno podría parar a tiempo el golpe, o esquivarlo! " [907]. Familiar with the extent of Doña Concha's manipulation of Tadeo, the reader perceives that the observation applies equally to Tadeo, led blindly by her first to poison and then to shoot Bocanegra. All of the characters in *Muertes de perro* march blindly and irrevocably toward their fate, drawn by their passions. While from the vantage point of hindsight Pinedo can observe of the manner of Doña Concha's death, "hay casos en que hubiera sido menester casi un milagro para torcer destino tan perfectamente previsible, dadas las circunstancias" [863], in truth the workings of fate are clearly visible only to the distanced observer. Pinedo fails to detect the guiding hand of fate in his own life, but his observation does underscore the consistency of human behavior from which he cannot escape.

Pinedo describes his fellow travelers in his opening pages in terms which disassociate him from their involvement in the course of events: "Ellos pugnan, ellos luchan, ellos se desgarran, ellos se arrancan la vida y, movidos por oleadas de ciega pasión, actúan como protagonistas" [858]. The ultimate irony of *Muertes de perro* is that Pinedo, the narrator-observer becomes himself a protagonist, a narrator-agent swept up in a wave of blind passion; the man who not altogether believably proclaims of the hero's role, "desde luego renuncio a semejante gloria" [857], in the end envisions himself as a grateful nation's savior [1017]. In short, the reader, primed by Pinedo's own verbal ironies and elucidation of situational ironies is in a position to view Pinedo from the start in an ironic context in which he, who casts himself as a man apart, distinct from and better than other men, reveals himself to be of the same stuff. This superior perspective the reader shares with the implied author. Insofar as Pinedo elucidates the irony of human existence in the lives of others, he is a reliable narrator, a spokesman for the implied author; but insofar as he remains blind to the ironies of his own existence, his perspective is limited.

Whereas Pinedo and Tadeo engage in verbal irony and point to the dramatized irony in the lives of others, José Lino Ruiz remains too close to his material in Parts I and III of *El fondo del vaso* to become an ironist. Nor does José Lino's acceptance of other men's words and actions at face value allow him to detect their ironies.[2] In this second novel irony functions mainly on the level of communication between reader and implied author, with the reader as the observer or detector of ironies and José Lino as principal victim. Whereas Pinedo is consciously ironic, José Lino consciously avoids an ironic stance [1032]; even when he envisions himself an ironist, in a plan of coldly detached behavior with which to confront Candy [1065], the reader immediately realizes he is incapable of acting out this calculated role.

In Part I of *El fondo del vaso* the discrepancy between the reader's interpretation of what José Lino records and his own interpretation allows the reader to detect José Lino's indirect, unconscious self-characterization. As Booth describes this technique:

> In the irony with which we are concerned, the speaker is himself the butt of the ironic point. The author and reader are secretly in collusion, behind the speaker's back, agreeing upon the standard by which he is found wanting.[3]

The narrator's impercipience, his inflated pride, his confidence in his social position — all reveal a different image from the one he consciously projects. This devastating Irony of Self-Betrayal, as Muecke terms it, which undercuts José Lino's self-presentation, maintains the reader at a consistent distance from the narrator despite his redeeming features which automatically guarantee him a degree of sympathy. In a blatant example of self-betrayal, José Lino enters the phrase "la donna è mobile" in his diary in reference to

---

[2] As already cited in Chapter III, José Lino notes on one occasion the "ironía maliciosa en las pupilas de todos" [1044] but fails to interpret its real significance.

[3] Booth, *Fiction,* p. 304.

Candy, terming it an "apotegma latino" [1097]; his error ironically betrays the extent of his ignorance instead of revealing his erudition. In addition to dramatized irony, *El fondo del vaso* contains a conscious ironist in the person of Rodríguez. Rodríguez offers an example of his covert verbal irony in pointedly reminding José Lino of the "escaso botín capturado por mí en dos días largos de ausencia, durante los cuales había dejado en mayor desamparo a esposa, negocios y amigos" [1037]. The irony passes undetected by its victim, who accepts only the visible truth of the charges, without perceiving the booty which Rodríguez has captured in his absence.

In an extended example of the irony of self-betrayal, the reader follows Rodríguez's affair with Corina through José Lino's unsuspecting eyes. His exaggerated praise of Rodríguez and his surprised pleasure at his friend's eventual willingness to aid him in vindicating Bocanegra, as well as his confused pleasure at Corina's support of the idea, lead the reader to recognize that there is more to the triangular situation than meets José Lino's gaze. Returning from the wild goose chase to San Cosme on which Rodríguez sent him, José Lino finds his mentor comfortably ensconced in an armchair and concludes: "por lo visto, había pasado casualmente a inquirir noticias de mi viaje" [1036]. By relying purely on visual evidence he fails to detect the calculation in Rodríguez's presence and remains ignorant of his own situation. Similarly, José Lino records Rodríguez's thoughtfulness in refraining from interrupting his workday, with the exception of a few calls inquiring whether José Lino will return home soon [1032]. While the narrator implicitly interprets such calls in a positive light, assuming that Rodríguez wishes to see him, the reader recognizes the narrator's ignorance of the fact that Rodríguez wishes to ensure privacy for a rendez-vous. Such examples of dramatized irony abound. When José Lino broaches the subject of compensating Rodríguez for his literary aid, his choice of words states the circumstances more clearly than he can know: "Al aludir yo por último, con la mayor delicadeza, a su posible retribución (compensación fue la palabra empleada por mí), saltó de inmediato, herida, la famosa dignidad española" [1025]. Well-compensated already by Corina, Rodríguez has indeed exacted retribution from José Lino. In an attempt at verbal discretion, José Lino unknowingly selects the appropriate description, underscoring for the reader the difference between the socially expected reaction and his superfluous offer of compensation.

But José Lino is not the sole victim of ironies in *El fondo del vaso*. The reader has little direct access to Corina, her state of mind being largely revealed through her actions as recorded by her uncomprehending husband. Thus the reader is rarely in a position to evaluate Corina. In one exception, Corina accuses José Lino of having forced her to adopt Penelope's strategem "de urdir y tramar" in his absence, a reference to her lies to Candy's father. The reader, recalling that "el arte de Penélope" was designed to keep suitors at a distance from the faithful wife of the wandering Greek, views Corina's invocation of Penelope's defense as an ironic contrast to her own actions. Corina's rhetorical "el arte de Penélope, ¿verdad?" [1069] receives resounding concurrence from the reader, but not in the sense in which she intends.[4]

The overall structure of *El fondo del vaso* also reveals the implied author as ironist. In an opposite reversal to that experienced by Pinedo at the end of *Muertes de perro,* José Lino passes from an unself-conscious narrator to a self-conscious, reliable narrator in the closing chapter of *El fondo del vaso*. By the time he sees himself for who he is, the realization has come too late, as he ultimately realizes:

> Siempre me pasa lo mismo, y para todo: tardo demasiado en reaccionar; y el caso es que la vida no da respiro... Soy lerdo, soy un bobo (saber que a uno lo tienen por bobo es una cosa, y otra muy distinta sentirse uno mismo bobo por dentro, como yo me siento ahora); soy un tontaina: siempre reacciono tarde. Ahí me quedé, hecho un pasmarote; ahí me estuve, duro como un poste. Y ella, claro está, tomó mi estolidez por orgullo... No hay remedio: esta vida es una comedia de las equivocaciones; un

---

[4] Hiriart has also commented upon this reference to Penelope, citing an additional irony in Corina's destruction of José Lino's carefully laid plans:

> según suele ocurrir en las obras de Ayala, la alusión literaria toma un sesgo irónico: la esposa de José Lino está lejos de tejer su tela en protección de su fidelidad conyugal; y, además, ese tejido pasa a ser metafóricamente el de la intriga. Corina deshace ante el preocupado padre de Candy la labor tramada por su marido y, a su vez, urde una nueva trama.

Las alusiones literarias, p. 101.

drama de las equivocaciones; una tragedia; una tragicomedia. Tampoco ella fue capaz de comprender nada de lo
que a mí me pasaba. [1175]

From his newly-gained perspective José Lino can present the irony
of his past situation directly, reinforcing the reader's distance from
the individual that José Lino was. As the allusion to Shakespeare's
A Comedy of Errors illustrates, Corina and José Lino have once
again completely misunderstood one another. José Lino makes plain
the irony of this situation: "Hubiera bastado un simple gesto mío,
ese pequeño gesto que tan vorazmente aguardaba; una migaja, una
nada; pero yo, estúpido, la dejé ir" [1176]. Now when José Lino
terms himself *lerdo, bobo, estúpido,* there is no question of the
irony of self-betrayal; his assessment accords not only with his
fellow characters' assessment but with that of the reader and implied author. In sharing the implied author's view of himself and
of life José Lino becomes a reliable narrator. The reader, although
still distanced from the petty individual depicted on the plane of
action, responds positively to the shift in the narrator's perspective
in the narrative present.

As a first-person narrator, José Lino cannot voice the implied
author's perspective directly, but in the closing pages of the novel
starting with the penultimate section and growing towards his discovery of the whole truth in the paragraph quoted above, his
monologue begins to merge with the implied author's stance. The
irony of events demonstrates on a broader plane that it is the fate
of humanity to be constantly misunderstood and misunderstanding;
hence each human is an essentially solitary being. The term "tragicomedy" which climaxes José Lino's characterization of life signals
the duality of the implied author's position towards the world of
the novel. The closing words summarize for the reader the implied
author's view of the human condition — God have mercy on
mankind struggling in the mire of human existence.

The label "tragicomedy" dates back to Francisco Ayala's first
novel, *Tragicomedia de un hombre sin espíritu*. In a novel published
thirty-three years later, Pinedo and Tadeo Requena comment on
life as a combination of tragedy and comedy. In Tadeo's words:
"En medio de los actos de tragedia se intercala de vez en cuando,
como en el teatro clásico, algún entremés bufo" [908]. The comic

interludes in Pinedo's narrative satirize the values and behavior of the society as, similarly, the newspaper articles in Part II of *El fondo del vaso*; all acquire a pathetic or tragic dimension in the context of the whole, as Pinedo once observes:

> Sobre el fondo de la situación desencadenada por [pequeñeces semejantes], anécdotas como la referida adquieren un sentido trágico; la frivolidad puede alcanzar dimensiones trágicas; puede tener el efecto de un bofetón o de un escupitajo. [927]

With these words Pinedo elucidates the structuring principle underlying both novels in which the comic element in the form of grotesque satire heightens the tragic dimension for the reader, while irony functions to draw together these opposing elements. In such observations Pinedo, like José Lino at the close of the later novel, voices the norms of the implied author and hence offers reliable commentary. The duality of possible perspectives again receives emphasis when Pinedo comments on an episode from Tadeo's diary: "Si no fuera por las consecuencias trágicas a que nos ha conducido, sería cosa de risa" [994]. What on the surface or from less than the required distance appears comic, when viewed from the implied author's perspective evinces the tragic condition of human life. The distanced, ironic perspective of the implied author embraces the narrators of both novels in its scope; they attain this same distance in turn only on limited occasions: Pinedo in viewing the lives of others, and José Lino after experiencing the distancing process of isolation from society and his former life. Whereas Pinedo and Tadeo grasp the elements of comedy and tragedy separately, José Lino voices the view that life is a synthesis of these elements, a tragicomedy. But the emphasis lies on the perspective from which life is viewed, and from the implied author's distanced perspective on his novelistic world, men die like dogs after struggling in the mire of human existence. The response he calls for is pity but not on a human level; recourse seems to lie only outside human hands.

CONCLUSION

The first chapter of this study raises certain questions concerning the nature of the reader's response to the first-person narration comprising *Muertes de perro* and *El fondo del vaso*. From the preceding examination of these novels it appears that in equating first-person narration with reader identification Francisco Ayala has greatly oversimplified the narrator-reader relationships of both novels.[1] By asserting that such identification occurs, Ayala has overlooked the interplay between conscious and unconscious narrators, between the narrator as observer and the narrator as actor, and indeed between the multiple narrative perspectives. As other critics have maintained concerning the reader response to first-person narration in contemporary literature:

> Because of the schism in the hero who affirms his identity by a self-analysis or by the self-declaration of the narrative *je,* the cliché notion that the first-person narration logically brings the reader into a form of identification becomes somewhat questionable. Critics such as Morrissette and Pouillon feel that the use of the *je* actually "tend de plus en plus justement à intervenir pour empêcher l'auto-identification." Pouillon specifies that "être 'avec' quelqu'un, ce n'est donc pas avoir de lui une conscience réfléchie, ce n'est pas le connaître, c'est avoir 'avec' lui la même conscience irréfléchie de soi." That is to say that the reader may more easily achieve a circumstantial identification if the fictional center of consciousness is expressed in an unreflexive manner or if the center as a subjectivity is translated as an implicit presence.[2]

---

[1] See Chapter I, note 22. *Mis mejores páginas,* p. 18.
[2] Tobin Harry Jones, "Narrative Point of View and Related Forms of Reader Involvement in the French Nouveau Roman," Diss. Univ. of Min-

As the previous chapters have detailed, José Lino Ruiz's unreflective self-presentation raises greater sympathy than Pinedo's more consciously controlled narrative, although the most sympathetic narrator in either novel, in large part due to external factors, is María Elena Rosales, whose self-reflective confession in combination with her youth and orphaned status draw the reader into identification. Further, Tadeo Requena's moment of honest self-appraisal at the end of his life also produces a degree of reader identification, as to an even greater extent does José Lino's similar self-confrontation at the end of *El fondo del vaso*. But in no case is total reader identification achieved, despite the degree of sympathy.

In *Muertes de perro* and *El fondo del vaso* reader-narrator identification is further thwarted by the ironic stance of the implied author which distances the reader from the novelistic world and its inhabitants. Ayala, on the other hand, maintains that no distance exists between the narrator and the reader-implied author tandem in his novels. This assertion ignores the extensive role of irony, especially the irony of self-betrayal throughout Part I and portions of Part III of *El fondo del vaso,* and the multiple structural ironies. In Ayala's words, with specific reference to *El fondo del vaso*:

> Se ha suprimido toda distancia: y esta conciencia [José Lino Ruiz] *inclusiva* solidariza al autor y al lector con los personajes ficticios. Al mirarlos, se miran a sí mismos como en un espejo, y quedan petrificados. Pues lo que ven — en maneras diversas — es su propia destitución en un mundo cuyos valores se han hecho inciertos o se han disipado. He ahí lo insufrible.[3]

While readers do not necessarily find themselves "hundidos en la común miseria," as Ayala suggests, the reader does position himself alongside the implied author's vision of mankind as "hundido en la común miseria."

Ayala's contention that a unified vision underlies a writer's entire creative production[4] is upheld in his own case to the extent of the unity of the worldview of the implied authors of his two

---

nesota 1969, p. 33. Quotations cited are from Morrissette, p. 156, and Jean Pouillon, *Temps et Roman* (Paris: Gallimard, 1946), p. 80.

[3] *Mis mejores páginas*, p. 19.
[4] See Chapter I, note 14. *Estructura*, p. 60.

novels. The consistency of the animal imagery, of the style, and of ironic tone links the two novels in a common vision, as has already been established, so that a unified perspective on mankind within the novelistic worlds emerges from the implied author's stance. In a letter to a critic disconcerted by the vision of mankind implicit in Ayala's fiction, the author wrote:

> ¿... no deberá atribuirse a las condiciones que nuestro tiempo le impone al humano vivir esa impresión — sin duda falsa, aunque tan generalizada — de que los pobladores de mis novelas son inhumanos, impresión que desplaza sobre ellos (sobre todos nosotros, macacos o perros; pobres gatos en definitiva) la crueldad de una situación espiritual que nos aflige y nos degrada? Nos degrada, en efecto, hacia lo animalesco, al privarnos del cobijo de un sistema coherente de valores ideales con evidencia incontrovertible, colocándonos en un estado de ansiedad cómico-patético.... Lo que mis personajes revelan, lo que yo hubiera querido al menos que reflejaran, no es una maldad especial, que no la hay en ellos, sino el desamparo en que se vive hoy.[5]

Here Ayala stresses again his contention that the author as a living being speaks through his works with a single and unique view of the world in which he lives. This dimension lies entirely outside the scope of the present study, which is concerned with identifying the voice of the implied author within the fiction itself. The implied author of both novels is for the reader more distant from the narrators and more ironically superior than Ayala acknowledges. Distance functions in both novels to convey the quality of the individual human effort to which Ayala makes reference and further to avoid a melodramatic tone which might otherwise infiltrate the episodes in which the hand of fate falls heavily on a character. The dominant animal imagery of "esta perra vida" [1010] and the dominant characterization "pobre gata" which runs throughout both novels (and is in itself ironic when applied by José Lino to Corina [1023]) further establishes the characters on a subhuman plane beneath the reader whose detection of the im-

---

[5] *Mis mejores páginas*, pp. 18-19. (The title of the collection of short stories published immediately prior to *Muertes de perro* is *Historia de macacos* [1952]; hence the reference to *macacos*.)

plied author's ironies in any case grants him superiority to the narrators. The predominance of this imagery and tone cannot be overcome even in the moment in which a narrator confronts his naked self, especially when, like José Lino, that narrator in turn subscribes to the imagery; the view of mankind is such that the reader remains suspiciously distanced from the narrator even at such a moment however much sympathy he may feel toward the narrative act at that moment. That is to say, while the reader feels sympathy for the narrator in the narrative present, he remains ironically distanced from the narrator as object on the plane of action. Nor is the reader predisposed to accept a reversal of José Lino's previous self; only the enormity of his present circumstances accounts for his new-found self-awareness. In short, Francisco Ayala, perhaps the most perceptive of contemporary Spanish critics and one of the most masterful manipulators of narrative perspective in the contemporary Spanish novel, has unfairly simplified the narrative complexity of his own masterpiece in his critical commentary.

The principal critics of Ayala's fiction who have undertaken to characterize the authorial presence, or to invoke Booth's terminology, the implied author, in one or both of Ayala's novels, clash in their reading of these novels. Jorge Enjuto, writing of *Muertes de perro,* finds the implied author occupying an "objective" position towards the novel, causing the reader to react against his dispassionate detachment by identifying with the role of the individual in the novelistic world:

> Al analizar nuestro sentimiento descubrimos que, a pesar de la aspereza de las situaciones, la crueldad se origina más en la perspectiva que en el contenido. El punto desde donde el autor contempla los acontecimientos que se desarrollan en el libro se nos presenta como neutro, objetivo, y libre de prejuicios valorativos. Esta objetividad frente a lo humano se nos convierte de pronto en inhumana en su sentido más literal; de ahí el sentimiento de crueldad que nos embarga. Pero no es una crueldad clara, no ya dirigida hacia los personajes o hacia nosotros, nos hiere porque sospechamos entre las palabras contenidos que no nos gusta conocer, o quizá mejor, reconocer.[6]

---

[6] Jorge Enjuto, "Notas sobre el sentido de la obra literaria de Francisco Ayala," *Asomante,* 16 (1960), 32.

Although Enjuto's description emphasizes the distance separating the implied author from the characters, his choice of the term "objective" is unfortunate. The concept of perspectivism, both as expressed by Pinedo and as evidenced through the structure of both novels, controverts this term; objectivity not only clashes with first-person narration, it is inconceivable within the framework of either novel. Nevertheless, his point about the absence of "prejuicios valorativos" has been borne out by the present study as well.

Gonzalo Sobejano goes even farther astray by projecting a note of hope beyond the framework of the novel itself in unsubstantiated optimism which ignores altogether the character of the implied author and, more specifically, the consistency of the worldview. Describing José Lino Ruiz the critic writes:

> Aunque en las últimas líneas le veamos "solo para siempre, solo y pataleando en el fango," adivinamos que esta crisis moral será el comienzo de su ascenso desde el fango hasta la superficie.[7]

Sobejano here presupposes a radical change in José Lino which is inconsistent both with the ironic view of mankind and with the dimensions of José Lino's character as presented throughout Part I. The irony of José Lino's self-awareness is precisely that it comes so late.

Enrique Pezzoni, on the other hand, reads the implied author's stance as distanced ironically from both the narration and the reader, whom Pezzoni characterizes as disconcerted and confused. In his view the reader does not travel with the implied author but becomes instead an object in his ironic vision. Although he finds no shared perspective between reader and implied author, Pezzoni does acknowledge the requirement of active participation by the reader:

> Los hechos ... pierden poco a poco realidad inmanente. Y es que el lector acaba preguntándose en qué plano habrá que buscarles esa realidad a que trascienden. Se cierra el libro y tiene uno la impresión de que Ayala, guarecido

---

[7] Gonzalo Sobejano, "Dos libros narrativos de Francisco Ayala," *Papeles de Son Armadans*, 32, No. 96 (March 1964), 346.

> tras sus disfraces lastimosos, se sonríe con sorna ante nuestro desconcierto. Nos ha dado las cifras, pero a nosotros corresponde el cuidado de encontrarles la clave.[8]

Irony holds the key to the communication between reader and implied author and the detection of these ironies grants the reader access to the implied author's perspective.

One of the most valuable of Spanish critics, Ricardo Gullón, provides the best summation of the implied author in *Muertes de perro,* reading the implied author's position from within the novel and situating the reader alongside the implied author. Gullón's point of departure is a comparison between *Tirano Banderas, El Señor Presidente,* and *Muertes de perro*:

> de los tres libros el más duro, irónico y desesperanzado es el de Francisco Ayala. Si no recuerdo mal, no hay en todo el volumen un personaje decente, un corazón puro. La impresión, al finalizar la lectura, es desoladora. He aquí un mundo donde la vida no tiene sentido. Cerrado, obsesionante, no ya carece de cielo, sino de luz y de aire respirable. Toda la maquinaria del universo funciona entre podredumbre y es, ella misma, miseria. No hay horizonte; no hay futuro. El hombre nunca ha parecido tan abyecto como en esta historia. ¿Podrá, tal vez, entreverse, lejos, un poco de claridad, algo que consienta dar alas a la esperanza? Yo diría que el mundo ayalesco no permite esos resquicios. Su visión es esencialmente pesimista, y la soltura de su prosa, el estilo, tan directo y claro; la facilidad con que se hilvanan las escenas, no hace sino más evidente y admisible el horror de la situación.[9]

Recognizing the ironic perspective of *Muertes de perro,* Gullón most clearly expresses the effect of distance on the worldview emerging from the novel and similarly from *El fondo del vaso.* In the latter novel, José Lino's own awareness of being "solo y pataleando en el fango" [1176] at the close of his monologue, brings this distanced, ironic vision into sharper focus for the reader, but

---

[8] Pezzoni, p. 91.
[9] Ricardo Gullón, "Francisco Ayala: *Muertes de perro,*" *La Torre,* 6, No. 24 (1958), 175.

it remains essentially the same perspective on humanity which confronts the reader in both novels. The implied author's control of the reader's response makes acceptance of this vision of humanity inescapable.

BIBLIOGRAPHY

An exhaustive bibliography of works by and about Francisco Ayala was initially compiled in 1962 by Keith Ellis in his Ph.D. dissertation, "The Narrative Art of Francisco Ayala," published in 1964 as *El arte narrativo de Francisco Ayala.* Later Estelle Irizarry updated and reorganized the Ayala bibliography in her 1970 Ph.D. dissertation, published in 1971 as *Teoría y creación literaria en Francisco Ayala.* In a 1972 collection of essays entitled *Los recursos técnicos en la novelística de Francisco Ayala,* Rosario Hiriart included a modified bibliography which again updated the editions and critical studies of Ayala's fiction. One year later, Andrés Amorós published a *Bibliografía de Francisco Ayala,* a further expansion of previous bibliographies but organized in a predominantly chronological manner and with the addition of previously uncited articles published by Ayala in Spain in the mid-1920's.

Given the availability of a recent bibliography of Francisco Ayala which draws together the successive expansions of earlier bibliographies, the following bibliography includes only: (I) selected works by Ayala, including those cited in the present study; (II) other works cited in this study; (III) works by Ayala not cited in the Amorós bibliography; and (IV) critical studies of Ayala's fiction not cited by Amorós.

I. Francisco Ayala: Selected Bibliography

Confrontaciones. Barcelona: Seix Barral, 1972.
Ensayos. Madrid: Aguilar, 1971.
España a la fecha. Buenos Aires: Sur, 1965.
Experiencia e invención (Ensayos sobre el escritor y su mundo). Madrid: Taurus, 1960.
"El fondo sociológico en mis novelas." *Cuadernos Hispanoamericanos,* No. 228 (Dec. 1968), pp. 537-47. Rpt. in *Ensayos,* pp. 573-87.
"Galdós entre el lector y los personajes." *Anales galdosianos,* 5 (1970), 5-13.
El hechizado. Buenos Aires: Emecé, 1944.
El jardín de las delicias. Barcelona: Seix Barral, 1971.
Letter. 3 May 1972.
Mis mejores páginas. Madrid: Gredos, 1965.
"Los narradores en las novelas de Torquemada." *La Nación,* 29 March 1970, Section 3, pp. 1, 3. Rpt. in *Cuadernos Hispanoamericanos,* Nos. 250-252 (Oct. 1970-Jan. 1971), pp. 374-81; and in *Ensayos,* pp. 990-1001.
"Nueva divagación sobre la novela." *Revista de Occidente,* 2.ª época, 18, No. 54 (Sept. 1967), 294-312.

Obras narrativas completas. México: Aguilar, 1969.
"Prólogo." In *Cuentos.* Salamanca: Anaya, 1966, pp. 5-10.
Realidad y ensueño. Madrid: Gredos, 1963.
Reflexiones sobre la estructura narrativa. Madrid: Taurus, 1970. Rpt. in *Ensayos,* pp. 385-430.
"La relación entre el autor, el lector y el personaje en la obra narrativa." Lecture at the Univ. of Minnesota, 23 May 1970.
"Valle-Inclán and the Invention of Character." In *Valle-Inclán Centennial Studies.* Ed. Ricardo Gullón. Austin: Univ. of Texas Press, 1969, pp. 27-40.

II. WORKS CITED

Amorós, Andrés. *Bibliografía de Francisco Ayala.* Syracuse: Centro de Estudios Hispánicos, Syracuse University, 1973.
———. "Prólogo." In Francisco Ayala. *Obras narrativas completas.* México: Aguilar, 1969, pp. 9-92.
Baquero Goyanes, Mariano. *Perspectivismo y contraste: De Cadalso a Pérez de Ayala.* Madrid: Gredos, 1963.
Booth, Wayne. "Distance and Point of View: An Essay in Classification." *Essays in Criticism,* 11 (1961), 60-79.
———. "Distance et Point de Vue. Essais de classification." *Poètique,* 4 (1970), 511-24.
———. "The Revival of Rhetoric." *PMLA,* 80, No. 2 (1965), 8-12. Rpt. in *Now Don't Try to Reason with Me.* Chicago: Univ. of Chicago Press, 1970, pp. 35-46.
———. *The Rhetoric of Fiction.* Chicago: Univ. of Chicago Press, 1961.
———. "*The Rhetoric of Fiction* and Poetics of Fiction." *Novel,* 1 (1967-1968), 106-17. Rpt. in *Now Don't Try to Reason with Me,* pp. 151-69.
———. *A Rhetoric of Irony.* Chicago: Univ. of Chicago Press, 1974.
Durrell, Lawrence. *The Alexandria Quartet: Justine, Balthazar, Mountolive, Clea.* 4 vols. London: Faber and Faber, 1957-1960.
Ellis, Keith. *El arte narrativo de Francisco Ayala.* Madrid: Gredos, 1964.
———. "The Narrative Art of Francisco Ayala." Diss. Univ. of Washington 1962.
———. Letter. 18 May 1972.
———. Rev. of *Teoría y creación literaria en Francisco Ayala,* by Estelle Irizarry. *Hispania,* 55 (1972), 970.
Enjuto, Jorge. "Francisco Ayala: *El fondo del vaso.*" *Asomante,* 20 (1964), 79-82.
Fitch, Brian T. "Aesthetic Distance and Inner Space in the Novels of Camus." *Modern Fiction Studies,* 10 (1964), 279-92.
———. *Narrateur et Narration dans "L'Etranger" d'Albert Camus, Analyse d'un fait littéraire.* 2nd ed. Les Archives des Lettres Modernes, No. 34. Paris: Lettres Modernes, 1968.
Foltz, David Allen. "Beyond Alienation in Four Contemporary American Novels." Diss. Univ. of Arizona 1974.
Frye, Northrop. *Anatomy of Criticism.* 1957; rpt. New York: Atheneum, 1965.
Gullón, Germán. "La retórica de Cortázar en *Rayuela.*" *Insula,* 26, No. 299 (Oct. 1971), 13.
Gullón, Ricardo. "Francisco Ayala: *Muertes de perro.*" *La Torre,* 6, No. 24 (1958), 173-76.

Hiriart, Rosario. *Las alusiones literarias en la obra narrativa de Francisco Ayala.* New York: Las Américas, 1972.

———. *Los recursos técnicos en la novelística de Francisco Ayala.* Madrid: Insula, 1972.

Humphrey, Robert. *Stream of Consciousness in the Modern Novel.* Berkeley: Univ. of California Press, 1954.

Iglesias Laguna, Antonio. *Treinta años de novela española, 1938-1968.* Vol. I. Madrid: Prensa Española, 1969.

Irizarry, Estelle. "Francisco Ayala: Relaciones entre su obra crítica y teórica con la de ficción." Diss. George Washington Univ. 1970.

———. *Teoría y creación literaria en Francisco Ayala.* Madrid: Gredos, 1971.

Iser, Wolfgang. *The Implied Reader: Patterns of Communication in Prose Fiction from Bunyan to Beckett.* Baltimore: The Johns Hopkins University Press, 1974.

Joly, Monique. "Sistemática de perspectivas en *Muertes de perro.*" *Cuadernos Hispanoamericanos,* No. 245 (May 1970), pp. 415-29.

Jones, Tobin Harry. "Narrative Point of View and Related Forms of Reader Involvement in the French Nouveau Roman." Diss. Univ. of Minnesota 1969.

Killham, John. "My Quarrel with Booth." *Novel,* 1 (1967-1968), 267-72.

Letter from Estelle Stinespring, Manager, Rights and Permissions, University of Chicago Press. 21 Aug. 1975.

Mainer, José-Carlos. "La primera persona narrativa en Francisco Ayala y Serrano Poncela." *Insula,* 22, No. 242 (Jan. 1967), 3-4.

———. "Prólogo" to Francisco Ayala, *Cazador en el alba y otras imaginaciones.* Barcelona: Seix Barral, 1971, pp. 7-37.

Marquand, John Phillips. *H. M. Pulham, Esquire.* Boston: Little, Brown, 1941.

Marra-López, José R. *Narrativa española fuera de España, 1939-1961.* Madrid: Guadarrama, 1963.

Martínez Bonati, Félix. *La estructura de la obra literaria.* Santiago: Univ. de Chile, 1960.

Molina, Rodrigo. "*Muertes de perro*: Triple dimensión." *Estudios.* Madrid: Insula, 1961, pp. 9-32.

Morrissette, Bruce. "De Stendhal à Robbe-Grillet: Modalités du 'Point de vue.'" *Cahiers de l'Association Internationale des Etudes Françaises,* No. 14 (March 1962), pp. 143-63.

Muecke, D. C. *The Compass of Irony.* London: Methuen, 1969.

———. *Irony.* The Critical Idiom, No. 13. London: Methuen, 1970.

Núñez, Antonio. "Francisco Ayala, más cerca." *Cuadernos para el Diálogo,* Extraordinario, No. 22 (Oct. 1970), pp. 46-49. Rpt. in Francisco Ayala. *Confrontaciones.* Barcelona: Seix Barral, 1972, pp. 71-82.

Ortega y Gasset, José. *Obras completas.* Vols. II, III. Madrid: Revista de Occidente, 1946-1947.

Pérez de Ayala, Ramón. *Belarmino y Apolonio.* Madrid: Calleja, 1921.

———. *Troteras y danzaderas.* Madrid: Biblioteca Renacimiento, 1913.

Pezzoni, Enrique. "Francisco Ayala: La novela de la responsabilidad." *Sur,* No. 284 (Sept.-Oct. 1963), pp. 88-93.

Romberg, Bertil. *Studies in the Narrative Technique of the First-Person Novel.* Trans. Michael Taylor and Harold H. Borland. Lund, Sweden: Almquist and Wiksell, 1962.

Sanz Villanueva, Santos. *Tendencias de la novela española actual (1950-1970)*. Madrid: Cuadernos para el Diálogo, 1972.
Schnitzler, Arthur. *"None But the Brave"* [Trans. of *Leutnant Gustl*]. Trans. Richard L. Simon. In *Viennese Novelettes*. New York: Simon and Schuster, 1925, pp. 393-433.
Sobejano, Gonzalo. "Dos libros narrativos de Francisco Ayala." *Papeles de Son Armadans*, 32, No. 96 (March 1964), 343-48.
Valle-Inclán, Ramón María del. *Luces de Bohemia*. 1924; rpt. Madrid: Espasa-Calpe, 1961.
Warren, Robert Penn. *All the King's Men*. New York: Harcourt, Brace, 1946.
Wiseman, Cecile Craig Fitzgibbon. "*The Lamb's Head*: A Translation and Critical Study." Diss. Univ. of Texas 1971.
Worcester, David. *The Art of Satire*. 1940; rpt. New York: Norton, 1969.

III. FRANCISCO AYALA: RECENT WORKS

"La batalla nabal: *El Buscón*, de Quevedo." In *El comentario de textos*. Vol. I. Madrid: Castalia, 1973, pp. 79-86.
Cervantes y Quevedo. Barcelona: Seix Barral, 1974.
"Comentarios textuales a 'El Aleph' de Borges." *Explicaciones de Textos Literarios*, 2 (1973), pp. 3-7.
"La disputa de las escuelas críticas." In *The Analysis of Hispanic Texts: Current Trends in Methodology*. Ed. Mary Ann Beck, et al. Jamaica, N.Y.: Bilingual Press, 1976, pp. 1-5.
El escritor y su imagen (Ortega y Gasset, Azorín, Valle-Inclán, Antonio Machado). Madrid: Guadarrama, 1975.
"La gallina ciega." *Insula*, 28, Nos. 320-321 (July-Aug. 1973), 1, 3.
"Incidente." *Diálogos* [Mexico], No. 68 (March-April 1976), pp. 11-12.
"Inquisidor y rabino." *La Nación*, 14 July 1974, Section 3. Rpt. in "No hay mundo que lo sea." *Diálogos* [Mexico], No. 58 (July-Aug. 1974), p. 19.
"Intervención de Francisco Ayala." In *Novela española actual*. Madrid: Fundación Juan March - Cátedra, 1977, pp. 33-41.
"La invención literaria (A propósito de 'Incidente')." *Diálogos* [Mexico], No. 68 (March-April 1976), pp. 12-13.
"Lake Michigan." *El Urogallo*, 5, Nos. 27-28 (May-Aug. 1974), 7-8.
"Lección ejemplar." *Diálogos* [Mexico], No. 6 (Oct.-Nov. 1966), pp. 7-8.
"Man and Mask." In *Ramón del Valle-Inclán: An Appraisal of His Life and Works*. Ed. Anthony N. Zahareas, et. al. New York: Las Américas, 1968, pp. 40-42.
"Una mañana en Sicilia." *Papeles de Son Armadans*, 68, No. 203 (Feb. 1973), 210-14.
"La niña de oro." *Insula*, 31, No. 359 (Oct. 1976), 16.
"No hay mundo que lo sea: Todos los libros son inmorales, Sobre el trono, ¿Cuál es el sexo de los ángeles?" *Revista de Occidente*, 2.ª serie, No. 128 (Nov. 1973), 159-68.
"No hay mundo que lo sea: Todo el año (literalmente) carnaval, Caza de brujas, Inquisidor y rabino, Todo amor es fantasía." *Diálogos* [Mexico], No. 58 (July-Aug. 1974), pp. 17-19.
"Nota al centenario de Valle-Inclán." *Insula*, 21, Nos. 236-237 (July-Aug. 1966), 5.
La novela: Galdós y Unamuno. Barcelona: Seix Barral, 1974.

"Ortega y Gasset: Crítico literario." *Revista de Occidente,* 2.ª serie, 47, No. 140 (Nov. 1974), 214-35. Rpt. in *El escritor y su imagen,* pp. 13-38. Rpt. "Ortega y Gasset, Literary Critic." *Critical Inquiry,* 1 (1974-1975), 395-414. Also rpt. "Ortega y Gasset: Critique littéraire." *Etudes Littéraires,* 8, Nos. 2/3 (Aug.-Dec. 1975), 345-69.

"Un poema y la poesía de Antonio Machado." *La Torre,* Nos. 45-46 (Jan.-June 1964), 313-19. Rpt. in *El escritor y su imagen,* pp. 98-106.

"Reflexiones sobre la estructura narrativa: La ficcionalización del autor." *La Nación,* 29 June 1969, Section 4, pp. 1, 3. Rpt. in *Reflexiones sobre la estructura narrativa,* pp. 18-29.

"Un sueño." *La Nación,* 8 July 1973, Section 3, p. 8.

"Tomás Mann en varios tiempos." *La Nación,* 21 Sept. 1975, Section 3, pp. 1-2. Rpt. in *Revista de Occidente,* 3.ª serie, No. 1 (Nov. 1975), 19-27. Also rpt. in *El Urogallo,* 4, No. 34 (July-Aug. 1975), 65-75.

"Violación en Nueva York." *Insula,* 32, Nos. 368-369 (July-Aug. 1977), 40.

IV. CRITICAL STUDIES OF AYALA'S FICTION: AN UPDATING

Amorós, Andrés. "Las narraciones de Francisco Ayala." In *Novela española actual.* Madrid: Fundación Juan March - Cátedra, 1977, pp. 11-31.

Aranguren, José Luis L. "La evolución espiritual de los intelectuales españoles en la emigración." *Cuadernos Hispanoamericanos,* No. 38 (Feb. 1953), pp. 123-57.

Blanco Amor, José. "América en la narrativa de Francisco Ayala." *La Nación,* 7 Dec. 1969, Section 4, pp. 1-2. Rpt. in *Cuadernos Hispanoamericanos,* No. 247 (July 1970), pp. 269-73.

Boring, Phyllis Zatlin, Ed. *El rapto, by Francisco Ayala.* New York: Harcourt, 1966, pp. vii-xii.

Cano, José Luis. *Españoles de dos siglos.* Madrid: Seminarios y Ediciones, 1975.

Ellis, Keith. "*El Diablo Mundo* en 'Fragancia de Jazmines,' de Francisco Ayala." *Cuadernos Hispanoamericanos,* No. 283 (Jan. 1974), pp. 146-58.

Ferreras, Juan Ignacio. *Tendencias de la novela española actual, 1931-1969, seguidas de un catálogo de urgencia de novelas y novelistas de la posguerra española.* Paris: Ediciones Hispanoamericanas, 1970, pp. 107-08.

Foltz, David Allen. "Beyond Alienation in Four Contemporary American Novels [Francisco Ayala, *El fondo del vaso;* John Updike, *Couples;* Mario Vargas Llosa, *La casa verde;* Moacir Lopes, *A Ostra e o Vento*]." Diss. Univ. of Arizona 1974.

Garasa, Delfín Leocadio. "La condición humana en la narrativa española contemporánea." *Atenea,* 43 (1966), 109-38.

Guerrero, Obdulia. "El escritor y su obra." *La Torre,* Nos. 75-76 (Jan.-June 1972), 11-35.

Gullón, Ricardo. "Carta de España — Literatura a la deriva." *Realidad,* 4, No. 12 (Nov.-Dec. 1948), 343-49.

Hiriart, Rosario. "Conversación con Francisco Ayala." *Insula,* 31, No. 355 (June 1976), 3.

―――. "Notas sobre *Pantaleón y las visitadoras* y *El fondo del vaso.*" *Insula,* 29, No. 331 (June 1974), 16.

―――. Rev. of *Francisco Ayala. El rapto, Fragancia de jazmines, Diálogo entre el amor y un viejo,* ed. Estelle Irizarry. *Insula,* 30, No. 341 (April 1975), 8.

BIBLIOGRAPHY 133

Irizarry, Estelle. "La cultura como experiencia viva en *El jardín de las delicias* de Francisco Ayala." *Papeles de Son Armadans,* 68, No 204 (March 1973), 249-61.

―――. *Francisco Ayala.* Boston: Twayne, 1977.

―――, ed. *Francisco Ayala. El rapto, Fragancia de jazmines, Diálogo entre el amor y un viejo.* Textos Hispánicos Modernos, 31. Barcelona: Labor, 1974.

Jones, Margaret E. W. Rev. of *Las alusiones literarias en la obra narrativa de Francisco Ayala* and *Los recursos técnicos en la novelística de Francisco Ayala,* by Rosario Hiriart. *Hispanic Review,* 42 (1974), 115-17.

Luzuriaga, Jorge. "Francisco Ayala: *La cabeza del cordero.*" *Realidad,* 6, Nos. 17-18 (Sept.-Dec. 1949), 313-19. [Luzuriaga did not write the review of *Los usurpadores* for *Realidad* as cited by Amorós; see instead Fryda Schultz de Mantovani. "Francisco Ayala: *Los usurpadores.*" *Realidad,* 5, No. 15 (May-June 1949), 363-65.]

Martínez Cachero, José María, Francisco Ayala, and Andrés Amorós. "Coloquio." In *Novela española actual.* Madrid: Fundación Juan March - Cátedra, 1977, pp. 43-62.

Mermall, Thomas. "Sentido y función del bufón en *El fondo del vaso* de Francisco Ayala." *Insula,* 31, No. 359 (Oct. 1976), 5.

Molinari, María Angélica. "Distintas expresiones de la realidad americana: Valle-Inclán, Asturias, Ayala." *Revista de la Universidad Nacional de Córdoba,* 4 (1963), 115-26.

Murena, H. A. "Los penúltimos días." *Sur,* No. 175 (May 1949), pp. 65-66. [Discusses *Los usurpadores.*]

―――. "Los penúltimos días." *Sur,* No. 181 (Nov. 1949), p. 100. [Discusses *La cabeza del cordero.*]

Nora, Eugenio de. "Francisco Ayala. Con motivo de su 70 cumpleaños." *Humboldt,* 16, No. 59 (1976), 77-79.

Núñez Ladevéze, Luis. *Crítica del discurso literario.* Madrid: Cuadernos para el Diálogo, 1974.

Orozco Díaz, Emilio. "Una introducción al *Jardín de las delicias* de Ayala: Sobre Manierismo y Barroco en la narrativa contemporánea." In *Novela y novelistas: Reunión de Málaga 1972.* Málaga: Instituto de Cultura de la Diputación Provincial de Málaga, 1974, pp. 253-317.

Orringer, Nelson R. "Responsabilidad y evasión en *La cabeza del cordero* de Francisco Ayala." *Hispanófila,* No. 52 (Sept. 1974), pp. 51-60.

Rugg, Evelyn. Rev. of *Muertes de perro,* by Francisco Ayala. *Revista Interamericana de Bibliografía,* 11 (1961), 168-70.

Ruiz Copete, Juan de Dios. "Francisco Ayala o la unidad narrativa." *La Estafeta Literaria.* No. 486 (15 Feb. 1972), pp. 8-10.

NORTH CAROLINA STUDIES IN THE ROMANCE LANGUAGES AND LITERATURES

I.S.B.N. Prefix 0-8078-

Recent Titles

LI ROMANS DE WITASSE LE MOINE. *Roman du treizième siècle.* Édité d'après le manuscrit, fonds français 1553, de la Bibliothèque Nationale, Paris, par Denis Joseph Conlon. 1972. (No. 126). *-926-X.*

EL CRONISTA PEDRO DE ESCAVIAS. *Una vida del Siglo XV,* por Juan Bautista Avalle-Arce. 1972. (No. 127). *-927-8.*

AN EDITION OF THE FIRST ITALIAN TRANSLATION OF THE "CELESTINA," by Kathleen V. Kish. 1973. (No. 128). *-928-6.*

MOLIÈRE MOCKED. THREE CONTEMPORARY HOSTILE COMEDIES: *Zélinde, Le portrait du peintre, Élomire Hypocondre,* by Frederick Wright Vogler. 1973. (No. 129). *-929-4.*

C.-A. SAINTE-BEUVE. *Chateaubriand et son groupe littéraire sous l'empire.* Index alphabétique et analytique établi par Lorin A. Uffenbeck. 1973. (No. 130). *-930-8.*

THE ORIGINS OF THE BAROQUE CONCEPT OF "PEREGRINATIO," by Juergen Hahn. 1973. (No. 131). *-931-6.*

THE "AUTO SACRAMENTAL" AND THE PARABLE IN SPANISH GOLDEN AGE LITERATURE, by Donald Thaddeus Dietz. 1973. (No. 132). *-932-4.*

FRANCISCO DE OSUNA AND THE SPIRIT OF THE LETTER, by Laura Calvert. 1973. (No. 133). *-933-2.*

ITINERARIO DI AMORE: DIALETTICA DI AMORE E MORTE NELLA VITA NUOVA, by Margherita de Bonfils Templer. 1973. (No. 134). *-934-0.*

L'IMAGINATION POETIQUE CHEZ DU BARTAS: ELEMENTS DE SENSIBILITE BAROQUE DANS LA "CREATION DU MONDE," by Bruno Braunrot. 1973. (No. 135). *-934-0.*

ARTUS DESIRE: PRIEST AND PAMPHLETEER OF THE SIXTEENTH CENTURY, by Frank S. Giese. 1973. (No. 136). *-936-7.*

JARDIN DE NOBLES DONZELLAS, FRAY MARTIN DE CORDOBA, by Harriet Goldberg. 1974. (No. 137). *-937-5.*

MYTHE ET PSYCHOLOGIE CHEZ MARIE DE FRANCE DANS "GUIGEMAR", par Antoinette Knapton. 1975. (No. 142). *-942-1.*

THE LYRIC POEMS OF JEHAN FROISSART: A CRITICAL EDITION, by Rob Roy McGregor, Jr. 1975. (No. 143). *-943-X.*

THE HISPANO-PORTUGUESE CANCIONERO OF THE HISPANIC SOCIETY OF AMERICA, by Arthur Askins. 1974. (No. 144). *-944-8.*

HISTORIA Y BIBLIOGRAFÍA DE LA CRÍTICA SOBRE EL "POEMA DE MÍO CID" (1750-1971), por Miguel Magnotta. 1976. (No. 145). *-945-6.*

LES ENCHANTEMENZ DE BRETAIGNE. AN EXTRACT FROM A THIRTEENTH CENTURY PROSE ROMANCE "LA SUITE DU MERLIN", edited by Patrick C. Smith. 1977. (No. 146). *-9146-0.*

THE DRAMATIC WORKS OF ÁLVARO CUBILLO DE ARAGÓN, by Shirley B. Whitaker. 1975. (No. 149). *-949-9.*

A CONCORDANCE TO THE "ROMAN DE LA ROSE" OF GUILLAUME DE LORRIS, by Joseph R. Danos. 1976. (No. 156). *0-88438-403-9.*

POETRY AND ANTIPOETRY: A STUDY OF SELECTED ASPECTS OF MAX JACOB'S POETIC STYLE, by Annette Thau. 1976. (No. 158). *-005-X.*

FRANCIS PETRARCH, SIX CENTURIES LATER, by Aldo Scaglione. 1975. (No. 159).

STYLE AND STRUCTURE IN GRACIÁN'S "EL CRITICÓN", by Marcia L. Welles. 1976. (No. 160). *-007-6.*

MOLIERE: TRADITIONS IN CRITICISM, by Laurence Romero. 1974 (Essays, No. 1). *-001-7.*

When ordering please cite the *ISBN Prefix* plus the last four digits for each title.

Send orders to: University of North Carolina Press
Chapel Hill
North Carolina 27514
U. S. A.

NORTH CAROLINA STUDIES IN THE ROMANCE LANGUAGES AND LITERATURES

I.S.B.N. Prefix 0-8078-

Recent Titles

CHRÉTIEN'S JEWISH GRAIL. A NEW INVESTIGATION OF THE IMAGERY AND SIGNIFICANCE OF CHRÉTIEN DE TROYES'S GRAIL EPISODE BASED UPON MEDIEVAL HEBRAIC SOURCES, by Eugene J. Weinraub. 1976. (Essays, No. 2). -002-5.
STUDIES IN TIRSO, I, by Ruth Lee Kennedy. 1974. (Essays, No. 3). -003-3.
VOLTAIRE AND THE FRENCH ACADEMY, by Karlis Racevskis. 1975. (Essays, No. 4). -004-1.
THE NOVELS OF MME RICCOBONI, by Joan Hinde Stewart. 1976. (Essays, No. 8). -008-4.
FIRE AND ICE: THE POETRY OF XAVIER VILLAURRUTIA, by Merlin H. Forster. 1976. (Essays, No. 11). -011-4.
THE THEATER OF ARTHUR ADAMOV, by John J. McCann. 1975. (Essays, No. 13). -013-0.
AN ANATOMY OF POESIS: THE PROSE POEMS OF STÉPHANE MALLARMÉ, by Ursula Franklin. 1976. (Essays, No. 16). -016-5.
LAS MEMORIAS DE GONZALO FERNÁNDEZ DE OVIEDO, Vols. I and II, by Juan Bautista Avalle-Arce. 1974. (Texts, Textual Studies, and Translations, Nos. 1 and 2). -401-2; 402-0.
GIACOMO LEOPARDI: THE WAR OF THE MICE AND THE CRABS, translated, introduced and annotated by Ernesto G. Caserta. 1976. (Texts, Textual Studies, and Translations, No. 4). -404-7.
LUIS VÉLEZ DE GUEVARA: A CRITICAL BIBLIOGRAPHY, by Mary G. Hauer. 1975. (Texts, Textual Studies, and Translations, No. 5). -405-5.
UN TRÍPTICO DEL PERÚ VIRREINAL: "EL VIRREY AMAT, EL MARQUÉS DE SOTO FLORIDO Y LA PERRICHOLI". EL "DRAMA DE DOS PALANGANAS" Y SU CIRCUNSTANCIA, estudio preliminar, reedición y notas por Guillermo Lohmann Villena. 1976. (Texts, Textual Studies, and Translation, No. 15). -415-2.
LOS NARRADORES HISPANOAMERICANOS DE HOY, edited by Juan Bautista Avalle-Arce. 1973. (Symposia, No. 1). -951-0.
ESTUDIOS DE LITERATURA HISPANOAMERICANA EN HONOR A JOSÉ J. ARROM, edited by Andrew P. Debicki and Enrique Pupo-Walker. 1975. (Symposia, No. 2). -952-9.
MEDIEVAL MANUSCRIPTS AND TEXTUAL CRITICISM, edited by Christopher Kleinhenz. 1976. (Symposia, No. 4). -954-5.
SAMUEL BECKETT. THE ART OF RHETORIC, edited by Edouard Morot-Sir, Howard Harper, and Dougald McMillan III. 1976. (Symposia, No. 5). -955-3.
DELIE. CONCORDANCE, by Jerry Nash. 1976. 2 Volumes. (No. 174).
FIGURES OF REPETITION IN THE OLD PROVENÇAL LYRIC: A STUDY IN THE STYLE OF THE TROUBADOURS, by Nathaniel B. Smith. 1976. (No. 176). -9176-2.
A CRITICAL EDITION OF LE REGIME TRESUTILE ET TRESPROUFITABLE POUR CONSERVER ET GARDER LA SANTE DU CORPS HUMAIN, by Patricia Willett Cummins. 1977. (No. 177).
THE DRAMA OF SELF IN GUILLAUME APOLLINAIRE'S "ALCOOLS", by Richard Howard Stamelman. 1976. (No. 178). -9178-9.
A CRITICAL EDITION OF "LA PASSION NOSTRE SEIGNEUR" FROM MANUSCRIPT 1131 FROM THE BIBLIOTHEQUE SAINTE-GENEVIEVE, PARIS, by Edward J. Gallagher. 1976. (No. 179). -9179-7.
A QUANTITATIVE AND COMPARATIVE STUDY OF THE VOCALISM OF THE LATIN INSCRIPTIONS OF NORTH AFRICA, BRITAIN, DALMATIA, AND THE BALKANS, by Stephen William Omeltchenko. 1977. (No. 180). -9180-0.

When ordering please cite the *ISBN Prefix* plus the last four digits for each title.

Send orders to: University of North Carolina Press
Chapel Hill
North Carolina 27514
U. S. A.

NORTH CAROLINA STUDIES IN THE ROMANCE LANGUAGES AND LITERATURES

I.S.B.N. Prefix 0-8078-

Recent Titles

OCTAVIEN DE SAINT-GELAIS "LE SEJOUR D'HONNEUR", edited by Joseph A. James. 1977. (No. 181). *-9181-9.*

A STUDY OF NOMINAL INFLECTION IN LATIN INSCRIPTIONS, by Paul A. Gaeng. 1977. (No. 182). *-9182-7.*

THE LIFE AND WORKS OF LUIS CARLOS LÓPEZ, by Martha S. Bazik. 1977. (No. 183). *-9183-5.*

"THE CORT D'AMOR". A THIRTEENTH-CENTURY ALLEGORICAL ART OF LOVE, by Lowanne E. Jones. 1977. (No. 185). *-9185-1.*

PHYTONYMIC DERIVATIONAL SYSTEMS IN THE ROMANCE LANGUAGES: STUDIES IN THEIR ORIGIN AND DEVELOPMENT, by Walter E. Geiger. 1978. (No. 187). *-9187-8.*

LANGUAGE IN GIOVANNI VERGA'S EARLY NOVELS, by Nicholas Patruno. 1977. (No. 188). *-9188-6.*

BLAS DE OTERO EN SU POESÍA, by Moraima de Semprún Donahue. 1977. (No. 189). *-9189-4.*

LA ANATOMÍA DE "EL DIABLO COJUELO": DESLINDES DEL GÉNERO ANATOMÍSTICO, por C. George Peale. 1977. (No. 191). *-9191-6.*

RICHARD SANS PEUR, EDITED FROM "LE ROMANT DE RICHART" AND FROM GILLES CORROZET'S "RICHART SANS PAOUR", by Denis Joseph Conlon. 1977. (No. 192). *-9192-4.*

MARCEL PROUST'S GRASSET PROOFS. *Commentary and Variants,* by Douglas Alden. 1978. (No. 193). *-9193-2.*

MONTAIGNE AND FEMINISM, by Cecile Insdorf. 1977. (No. 194). *-9194-0.*

SANTIAGO F. PUGLIA, AN EARLY PHILADELPHIA PROPAGANDIST FOR SPANISH AMERICAN INDEPENDENCE, by Merle S. Simmons. 1977. (No. 195). *-9195-9.*

BAROQUE FICTION-MAKING. A STUDY OF GOMBERVILLE'S "POLEXANDRE", by Edward Baron Turk. 1978. (No. 196). *-9196-7.*

THE TRAGIC FALL: DON ÁLVARO DE LUNA AND OTHER FAVORITES IN SPANISH GOLDEN AGE DRAMA, by Raymond R. MacCurdy. 1978. (No. 197). *-9197-5.*

A BAHIAN HERITAGE. An Ethnolinguistic Study of African Influences on Bahian Portuguese, by William W. Megenney. 1978. (No. 198). *-9198-3.*

"LA QUERELLE DE LA ROSE: Letters and Documents", by Joseph L. Baird and John R. Kane. 1978. (No. 199). *-9199-1.*

TWO AGAINST TIME. *A Study of the very present worlds of Paul Claudel and Charles Péguy,* by Joy Nachod Humes. 1978. (No. 200). *-9200-9.*

TECHNIQUES OF IRONY IN ANATOLE FRANCE. Essay on *Les sept femmes de la Barbe-Bleue,* by Diane Wolfe Levy. 1978. (No. 201). *-9201-7.*

THE PERIPHRASTIC FUTURES FORMED BY THE ROMANCE REFLEXES OF "VADO (AD)" "PLUS INFINITIVE, by James Joseph Champion. 1978 (No. 202). *-9202-5.*

THE EVOLUTION OF THE LATIN /b/-/μ/ MERGER: A Quantitative and Comparative Analysis of the *B-V* Alternation in Latin Inscriptions, by Joseph Louis Barbarino. 1978 (No. 203). *-9203-3.*

METAPHORIC NARRATION: THE STRUCTURE AND FUNCTION OF METAPHORS IN "A LA RECHERCHE DU TEMPS PERDU", by Inge Karalus Crosman. 1978 (No. 204). *-9204-1.*

NARRATIVE PERSPECTIVE IN THE POST-CIVIL WAR NOVELS OR FRANCISCO AYALA "MUERTES DE PERRO" AND "EL FONDO DEL VASO", by Maryellen Bieder. 1979. (No. 207). 0-8078-*9207-6.*

RABELAIS: HOMO LOGOS, by Alice Fiola Berry. 1979. (No. 208). *-9208-4.*

When ordering please cite the *ISBN Prefix* plus the last four digits for each title.

Send orders to: University of North Carolina Press
 Chapel Hill
 North Carolina 27514
 U. S. A.

The Department of Romance Studies Digital Arts and Collaboration Lab at the University of North Carolina at Chapel Hill is proud to support the digitization of the North Carolina Studies in the Romance Languages and Literatures series.

www.ingramcontent.com/pod-product-compliance
Lightning Source LLC
Chambersburg PA
CBHW030237240426
43663CB00037B/1235